Cockney Ding Dong

COCKNEY DING DONG

CHARLES KEEPING

KESTREL BOOKS/EMI MUSIC PUBLISHING

*This book is dedicated to all the Trodd family,
at whose house in Vauxhall
most of the parties took place and most of
the songs were sung.*

*A selection of songs from this book is available on the record
issued on the Line Records label (no. 2032)*

KESTREL BOOKS
Published by Penguin Books Ltd
Harmondsworth, Middlesex, England
EMI MUSIC PUBLISHING LTD
138-140 Charing Cross Road, London WC2H 0LD

Selection, introduction and illustrations copyright © Charles Keeping, 1975
Music arrangements copyright © EMI Music Publishing Ltd, 1975
See also copyright notices on individual songs.

All rights reserved. No part of this publication may be reproduced, stored in a retrieval system, or transmitted in any form or by any means, electronic, mechanical, photocopying, recording, or otherwise, without the prior permission of the copyright owner.

First published 1975

ISBN 0 7226 5061 2

Set by London Filmsetters in 'Monophoto' Times 327

Printed in Great Britain by
Lowe & Brydone (Printers) Ltd, Thetford, Norfolk

Contents

Preface 7

COMIC SONGS

The Hobnailed Boots that Farver Wore	11
What a Mouth!	14
The Golden Dustman	18
'Alf a Pint of Ale	22
Down the Road	24
My London Country Lane	28
It's a Great Big Shame	32
Wot's the Good of Hanyfink! Why! Nuffink!	34
When the Old Dun Cow Caught Fire	37
The D.C.M.	43
If It Wasn't For the 'Ouses In Between	47
In the Shade of the Old Apple Tree	50
They're Moving Father's Grave to Build a Sewer	52
Wot Cher!	54
Where Did You Get That Hat?	58
They're All Very Fine and Large	61
On Monday I Never Go to Work	64
I'm Henery the Eighth, I Am!	67
Sing Me to Sleep	70
Boiled Beef and Carrots	72
A Comical Cock	74
The Moon Shines Tonight on Charlie Chaplin	76
The Amateur Whitewasher	78
I'm a Navvy	81
Feeding the Ducks on the Pond	82
When I Went for a Soldier	84

SENTIMENTAL SONGS

Liza, You Are a Lady	86
Liza, It's a Beautiful Starry Night	87
Liza Johnston	90
If Those Lips Could Only Speak	91
That's Where My Love Lies Dreaming	93
The Sunshine of Your Smile	96
Sons of the Sea	98
Granny	100
When the Summer Comes Again	102
Whilst the Dance Goes On	105
Jeerusalem's Dead!	107
Silver Bells	110
The Coster's Linnet	112
My Old Dutch	116
I Speak the Truth	118
The Song of the Thrush	122
A Sailor's Song	124
The Blind Boy	126
The Blind Irish Girl	129
Pal of My Cradle Days	132
For I'm Not Coming Home	134
That's What God Made Mothers For	137
As Your Hair Grows Whiter	140

KNEES-UP SONGS

Knees Up Mother Brown!	142	I've Got a Lovely Bunch of Coconuts	152
Any Old Iron?	146	When There Isn't a Girl About	154
Don't Dilly Dally on the Way	149	I Do Like to Be beside the Seaside	156
The Cokey Cokey	151		

ALTOGETHER SONGS

Green Gravel	161	Mademoiselle from Armentieres	170
Chase Me Charley	162	Two Lovely Black Eyes	172
The Naughty Sparrow	163	Maybe It's Because I'm a Londoner	174
Pack Up Your Troubles in Your Old Kit-Bag	164	Glorious Beer	176
Little Town in My Ould County Down	166	Come Inside, Yer Silly Bugger	179
It's a Long, Long Way to Tipperary	168	We All Came in the World with Nothing	180

PARTING SONGS

We All Go the Same Way Home	182	Memories	186
Fall In and Follow Me	184		
Index of Titles	189		
Index of First Lines	190		

Preface

All the songs in this book were sung at family parties or sing songs (or 'ding dongs', as most Londoners would call them). I was born and brought up in my maternal grandparents' house in Vauxhall Walk, Lambeth, London, and it was my mother's family who held these sing songs. My father, a one-time professional boxer, known as 'Charlie Clark of Lambeth', worked in the print on the old *Star* newspaper, and to the best of my knowledge his family never held such parties or sang at all.

To me these songs belonged to the family despite the fact that they came from many different sources: there were Victorian and Edwardian ballads, music hall comic songs, Great War songs, American songs and local parodies. My grandmother, who was born in Dorset, sang mostly ballads, while my grandfather, a sailor from Portsea, would sing about sailors and the sea with a fine tenor voice. I can't imagine 'Wot Cher!' without remembering Uncle Bob, 'A Comical Cock' belonged to Uncle Alf, and Aunt Em would sing the very Cockney:

Liza, it's a beautiful starry night,
Liza, the moon is shining bright.
I've come round to see if you'll elope,
Slip on something, if it's only a bar o' soap.

My father favoured songs about Ireland, such as 'Little Town in My Ould County Down'. My mother sang mostly children's songs. Then we had the action songs, like 'The D.C.M.', sung by Uncle Jim.

It was at the sing songs that all these songs came into their own. The sing songs were never common, rude or vulgar. Essentially family occasions, they were like a traditional play with a strict pattern, not unlike the old music hall.

Normally beginning around eight o'clock on a Saturday night, the front room or parlour would be ablaze with light. This room, rarely used except for parties, was filled with heavy, comfortable furniture, polished linoleum and deep pile carpets, Doulton pottery and photographs of relatives, soldiers and sailors, mostly long dead. There was a large overmantle over the fireplace and, of course, the most essential piece, an upright piano.

Bowls of cut glass held assorted nuts and chocolates, crisps and savoury biscuits; and there would be plenty of drink: a nine-gallon barrel of beer out in the passage, as well as stout, whisky, gin, port and sherry, with lots of lemonade for the children.

Paper hats, comic noses and glasses were given out as the families arrived. The parlour got very crowded, with the men standing, ladies sitting, and the children fighting. In the days of open fires, it was common practice for some of the men to 'black up': they took a little soot on to their fingers, and drew moustaches, beards and eyebrows on their faces. One uncle would red his nose with a ladies' lipstick.

There was lots of talking and shouting, mostly about football and boxing, confinements and operations. It wasn't strange to hear trade-union arguments from men wearing comic noses or to see a recently bereaved aunt dressed in black, but with a silly little paper hat on, eating a pickled onion.

Uncle Jack would sit down at the piano and start to play – general tunes to begin with: 'Lily of Laguna', 'I'll Take You Home again Kathleen', 'South of the Border'.

A shout would go up 'Order, please, Uncle Harry will start the singing'. He would walk to the piano protesting but with the family clapping and encouraging – he would always sing, of course.

All the singers in turn acted the same and then went to the piano. Only elderly ladies could sing from where they were sitting. Each person sang the same song or group of songs at every party. They never changed their repertoire, nor could anyone else sing their songs. When a member of the family died, he would always be remembered at these sing songs, because his songs would be sung by everyone in chorus, and he would be talked about and even tears shed on his behalf. That was the tradition.

Each singer performed alone, but all the company joined in the second chorus. The children could also perform, normally singing a song recently learned at school. Later, they would get their own song from wherever they chose. We had a lot of Bing Crosby's and Vera Lynn's.

When all the solo singing was over, Uncle Jack would go into a 'Knees up' routine, the carpets were pushed back, and all the company, except the very elderly, assembled in the middle of the room, either in a circle or in two lines, with their arms linked. Many a matronly aunt would dance separately holding a small favoured child. The tunes to which they danced were played without any break: 'Knees up Mother Brown', 'My Old Man', 'Sons of the Sea', 'When There Isn't a Girl About'. They would form a crocodile and go around the house, up and down the stairs, to such tunes as 'Fall In and Follow Me', and 'Let's All Go down the Strand'. On returning to the parlour they would form up again into a circle and finish off with 'The Cokey Cokey' and 'Under the Spreading Chestnut Tree'.

When the piano stopped, everyone would go for food, to a table laden with cold beef, cold pork and full ham, celery, watercress, radishes and beetroot; bread, butter and cheeses; pickled onions, walnuts, cauliflower and gherkins.

While the ladies were washing up, the piano would start again and the whole company sang old favourites as well as the latest popular songs: 'Show Me the Way to Go Home', 'We All Go the Same Way Home', 'After the Ball' and 'Daisy, Daisy'.

Tea was then handed round and the sing song slowly broken up, though perhaps there would be a few more solos. When the time came for going home and the coats had appeared, people went around kissing each other goodbye.

That was the pattern of it; there were no shocks or surprises, just a great sense of feeling a part of something.

These sing songs carried on through the Second World War, and we had many during the worst of the Blitz in Kennington, where we had moved in 1936. Sometimes the pianist would be asked to stop playing so that we could hear if the bombers were still overhead. Every time a serving member of the family came home on leave it would call for a ding dong, and 'a gallon, a man', as Uncle Alf used to say.

After the war things slowly changed: families moved out to the suburbs or into the new high-rise flats as the old houses were pulled down, and this stopped many of the parties and sing songs.

My family was no exception. They still get together at Christmas and sing the old songs, but as the old folks die off, the singing gets less, because the young ones prefer the record player. Only the 'Knees up' persists.

Many of the songs in this book were only ordinary popular songs in their time, but they lived, because people liked to sing. I hope that tradition continues.

And as I conclude, I have just heard of the sad death of my Uncle Jack Trodd at the age of seventy-two. He was the family piano player. He never sang, but he knew all the tunes by heart. We have no other pianist, so maybe as far as we are concerned the 'ding dong' ends here.

COMIC SONGS

The Hobnailed Boots that Farver Wore

1 Poor Farver's feet took up half the street,
   So his boots were in proportion,
   And the kids he'd squash in a day, by gosh!
   It really was a caution!

   Now me and my brother, from the age of four
   Up till eleven, used to sleep and snore
   Nice and cosy in a box of straw
   In the hobnailed boots that my Farver wore.

2 On a Lord Mayor's Day, just to shout hooray!
   Farver went and how he sauced 'em!
   But he blocked the street with his big flat feet,
   And the Lord Mayor drove acrosst 'em.

   And as he went ariding through the Guildhall door,
   Farver fell wallop on his back – oh lor!
   And the crowd stopped hoor'aying then, for all they saw
   Were the hobnailed boots that my Farver wore.

3 I've got good teeth and it's my belief
   I must thank my Farver for it,
   For if we've got coke and we want it broke,
   I pick it up and gnaw it.

   You've all got to eat a peck of dirt or more
   Before you snuff it, it's a wise old saw!
   Well I've had my whack, I cut me teeth – oh lor!
   On the hobnailed boots that my Farver wore.

4 When young Kate and Flo went to Southend, so
   As money they'd be saving,
   Farver's boot was seen as a bathing machine,
   In it, they undressed for bathing.

   While they were undressing, they forgot, I'm sure,
   The hole Farver'd cut for his corn – oh lor!
   Now the boys are agiggling at what they saw
   In the hobnailed boots that my Farver wore.

5 We had a goat with a cast-iron throat,
   Though he never used to bite us.
   Farver's boots he chewed, and that goat they slewed,
   For he died of appendicitus.

   Now that goat had whiskers, and they touched the floor,
   And when they were plaited by the kids next door,
   Made the finest laces that you ever saw
   For the hobnailed boots that my Farver wore.

THE HOBNAILED BOOTS THAT FARVER WORE

Copyright 1907 by FRANCIS, DAY & HUNTER LTD., London.

WHAT A MOUTH!

1. Jimmy Binks would be a handsome feller
   If he had another face and a diff'rent smeller,
   But his mouth queers him from winning in a beauty show;
   For it looks just like a steam-boat funnel,
   Or a railway arch, or the Blackwall tunnel,
   And you can't see Jim when he opens it wide, you know.
   And when poor Jim goes walking about
   You can hear the kids all hollaring out.

   What a mouth! what a mouth! what a 'north and south'!
   Ker-i-key! What a mouth he's got!
   When he was a youngster, oh! Lord Lovell,
   Why, his poor old mother used to feed him with a shovel.
   What a gap! poor chap! he's never been known to laugh,
   For if he did it's a penny to a quid
   That his face'd fall in half!

2. Though his great big mouth it ain't all honey,
   He can whisper in his own ear, ain't it funny?
   But to lay the dust he has to drink a lot, oh, my!
   And he got so tight one foggy morning
   That he laid down flat in the roadway yawning,
   As a poor old man was delivering coals near by.
   And as he went to shift the load,
   He saw Jim's mouth out in the road.

   What a mouth! what a mouth! what a 'north and south'!
   Ker-i-key! What a mouth he's got!
   The coalman, an old short-sighted feller,
   Saw his mouth wide open, and he took it for the cellar,
   And he shot the lot right into his mouth, no joke!
   For Jim, poor soul, 's got a tummy full of coal,
   And he coughs up lumps of coke!

3. In the top room of the 'Rose and Thistle'
   Jimmy often has a try to wet his whistle,
   But he can't succeed until he's had a hundred 'pots'.
   First a hundred pots of beer he'll swallow,
   Then as all his teeth at the back are hollow,
   He can still find room for a dozen or so 'rum hots'.
   A new barmaid came there one night,
   She saw Jim's face and yelled with fright.

   What a mouth! what a mouth! what a 'north and south'!
   Ker-i-key! What a mouth he's got!
   He opened it wide and the barmaid hollared,
   For a pewter pot he had accidentally swallowed.
   It was hot, that pot soon melted and now he sits
   Down by the fire with a little bit o' wire,
   And he hooks up two bob bits.

4. Jimmy's wife had such a lovely baby,
   With a mouth as big as Jim's, or larger, maybe,
   And I shan't forget the morning that he cut one tooth,
   When the poor young ma heard baby blubber
   For a nice hard teat that was made of rubber,
   She at once took him to the chemist, and, it's the truth,
   They could not get inside the door
   Till they shut that baby's mouth – oh, lor!

What a mouth! what a mouth! what a 'north and south'!
Ker-i-key! What a mouth he's got!
'As baby's ateething,' said his mummy,
'Will you please, sir, let me have a penny rubber dummy?'
Said the cove, 'Bai Jove' as he sucked a big jujube,
'There's no rubber teat for a penny that'll fit,
He wants a twopenny tube.'

5 Jimmy Binks in bed one night was snoring,
And the neighbours round about thought a lion was roaring,
Then the old Dutch clock, that was hanging on the bedroom wall,
From the nail fell into his big mouth, wallop!
Jim woke, and yelled, 'Go for Doctor Jalap!'
Said his wife, 'No fear! you have swallowed the clock, that's all.'
And now the people, isn't it fine?
Look down in his throat to see the time.

What a mouth! what a mouth! what a 'north and south'!
Ker-i-key! What a mouth he's got!
The works of the old Dutch clock keep whizzing
In his 'rum-tum-tum-my' like a lot of sherbet fizzing,
And his wife, what strife!, can't sleep of a night, that's right!
'Cause against his 'tum' she can hear the pendulum
Going tock-tock-tick all right.

The Golden Dustman

1 Me and old Bill Smiff's bin dust-'oys,
Allus work'd the same old rahnd;
Strange to say we've struck a Klondyke,
And we've shared the welf we fahnd.
'Ow it 'appen'd, there's a miser,
'Ud never let us shift 'is dust—
A Toosday night 'e died, and Wensday,
Like two burglars in we bust;
Gets to work, and bless yer eye-sight,
OH! such welf yer never saw—
'Apeneys, fardens, lor, in fousands!
And to fink that last week I was poor!

But nah I'm goin' to be a reg'lar toff,
A ridin' in my carriage and a pair;
A top 'at on my 'ed, and fevvers in my bed,
And call meself the dook o' Barnet Fair;
As-terry-my-can rahnd the bottom o' my coat,
A Piccadilly winder in my eye;
Ah, fancy all the dustmen a-shoutin' in my yer,
'Leave us in yer will before yer die!'

2 Stuck inside a rusty saucepan,
    Wot looked a worn-out mat;
    Close in-spec-shun, 'twas a stocking,
    Full o'nuggets – big as that!
    Down we flops upon our knees-ses,
    See my scoopin' up the welf,
    When up I jumps, oh! oh! so happy,
    'Ardly could believe me-self,
    The guvnor just nah sez, 'Come, 'Iggins,
    'Ere, get to work, yer looks 'arf tight.'
    'Get to wot, 'ere, who yer kiddin'?
    Yer can dine wiv me next Sunday night!'

3 In the summer I'll go yachting,
    With the Dooks and the Em-per-ors;
    In the autumn spot yer 'umble
    Shooting Grashes on the moors,
    What price me a-drivin' tandem,
    Wiv a cahntess by me side?
    If she likes to pop the question,
    Well, I'll consent to be 'er bride.
    As for low in-sin-u-a-tions
    As regards my style and sich,
    Well, I'll soon teach 'em ettiketty,
    If I slaps this 'crost their snitch.

THE GOLDEN DUSTMAN

Words by Eric Graham. Music by George le Brunn

This arrangement © 1975 by BRITISH AND CONTINENTAL MUSIC AGENCIES LTD.

'Alf a Pint of Ale

Copyright by M. WITMARK & SON, London.

'ALF A PINT OF ALE

1 I 'ate those blokes wot talk about,
The fings wot they likes to drink,
Such as tea and corfee,
Cocoa and milk,
Of such fings I never fink.
I'm plain in me 'abits,
And I'm plain in me food
But wot I say is this,
A man wot drinks such rubbish with his meals,
Well I always gives him a miss.

Now for breakfast I never fink of 'aving tea,
I likes a 'arf a pint of ale,
For my dinner I likes a little bit o' meat,
And a 'arf a pint of ale.
For my tea I likes a little bit o' fish
And a 'arf a pint of ale,
And for supper I likes a crust o' bread and cheese,
And a pint and a 'arf of ALE!

2 Now this is how I looks at it,
And I think you'll agree with me,
I've never seen a man get drunk in me life,
On corfee, cocoa or tea.
You think I'll pay
One and eight a pound for tea?
Why the thought makes me feel queer;
When I think of what you'd get for another two and six,
Such a pretty little barrel of beer.

3 Now folks wot drink such stuff as that
Are always looking pale.
They've pains in their tummies
And they've pains in their backs,
But I never had a pain with ale.
I always feel happy, and I always feel right,
When I've had a glass or two,
So why should I drink corfee or tea,
When there's plenty of ale would do?

Down the Road

Words and music by Fred Gilbert

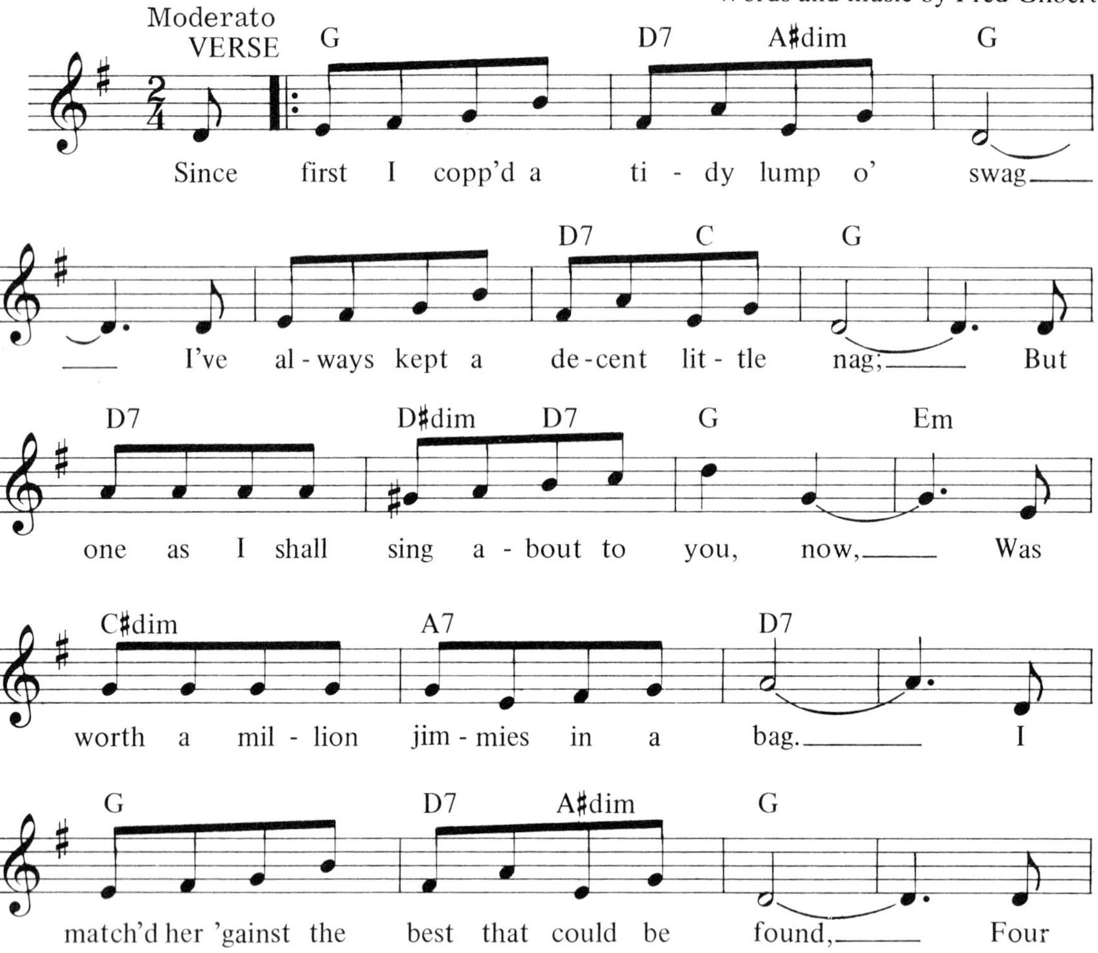
Moderato
VERSE
G D7 A♯dim G
Since first I copp'd a ti - dy lump o' swag
D7 C G
I've al - ways kept a de - cent lit - tle nag; But
D7 D♯dim D7 G Em
one as I shall sing a - bout to you, now, Was
C♯dim A7 D7
worth a mil - lion jim - mies in a bag. I
G D7 A♯dim G
match'd her 'gainst the best that could be found, Four

This arrangement © 1975 by BRITISH AND CONTINENTAL MUSIC AGENCIES LTD.

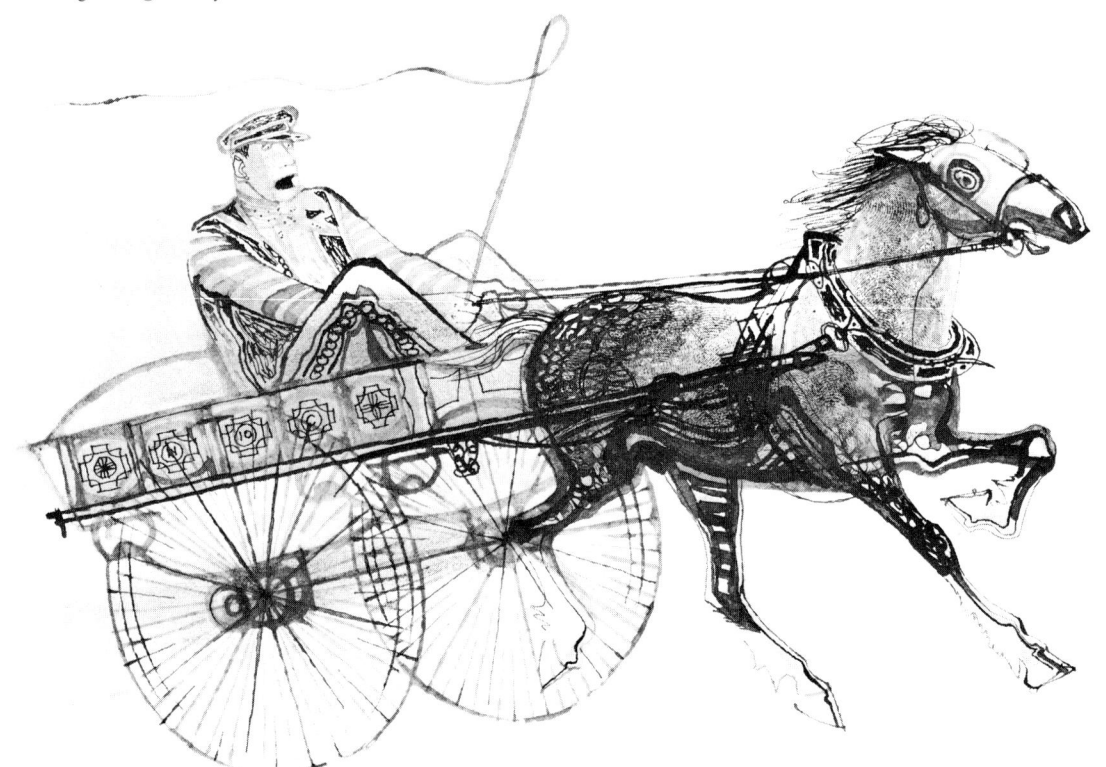

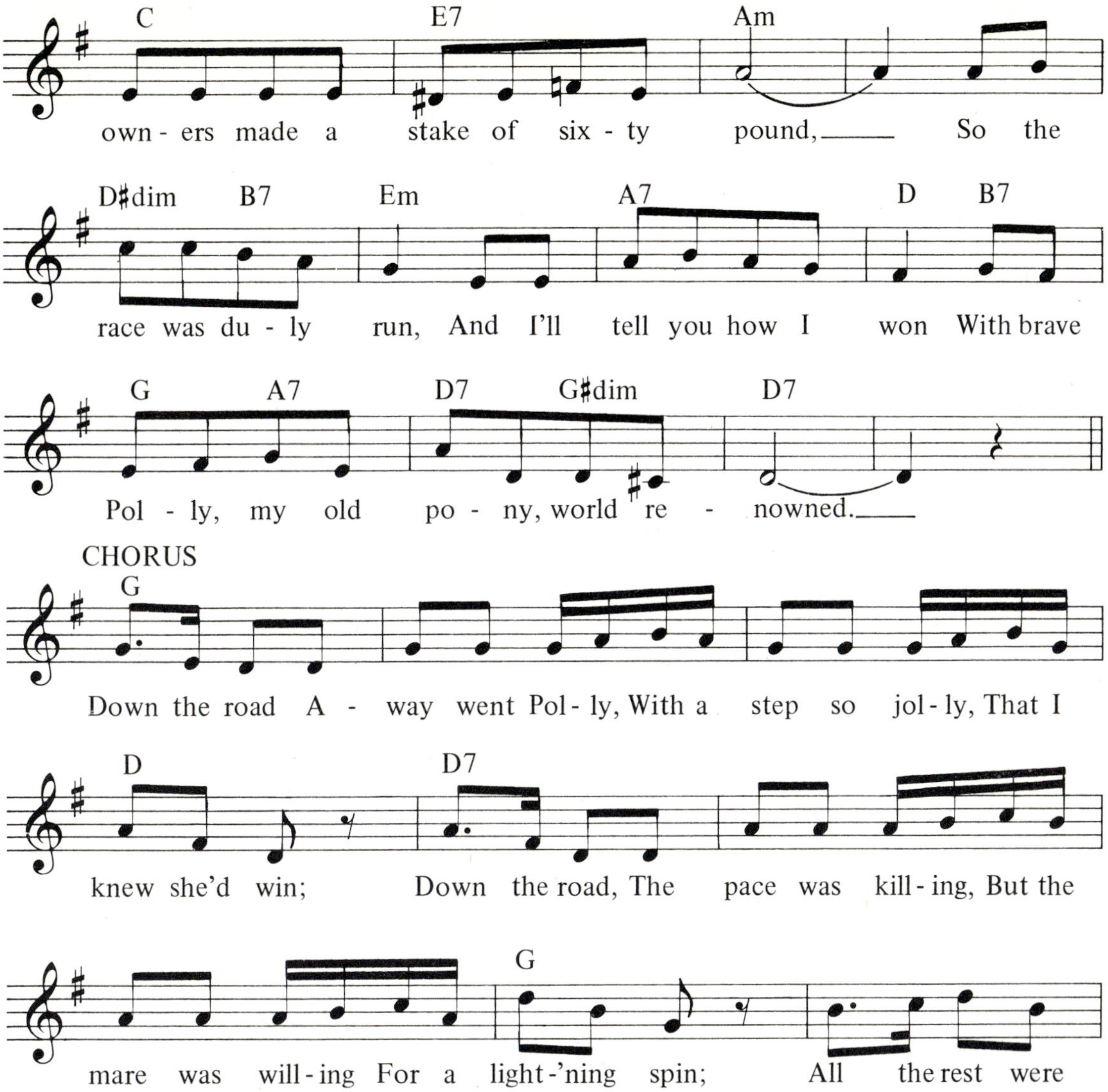
C E7 Am
own - ers made a stake of six - ty pound, So the
D♯dim B7 Em A7 D B7
race was du - ly run, And I'll tell you how I won With brave
G A7 D7 G♯dim D7
Pol - ly, my old po - ny, world re - nowned.
CHORUS
G
Down the road A - way went Pol - ly, With a step so jol - ly, That I
D D7
knew she'd win; Down the road, The pace was kill - ing, But the
G
mare was will - ing For a light-'ning spin; All the rest were

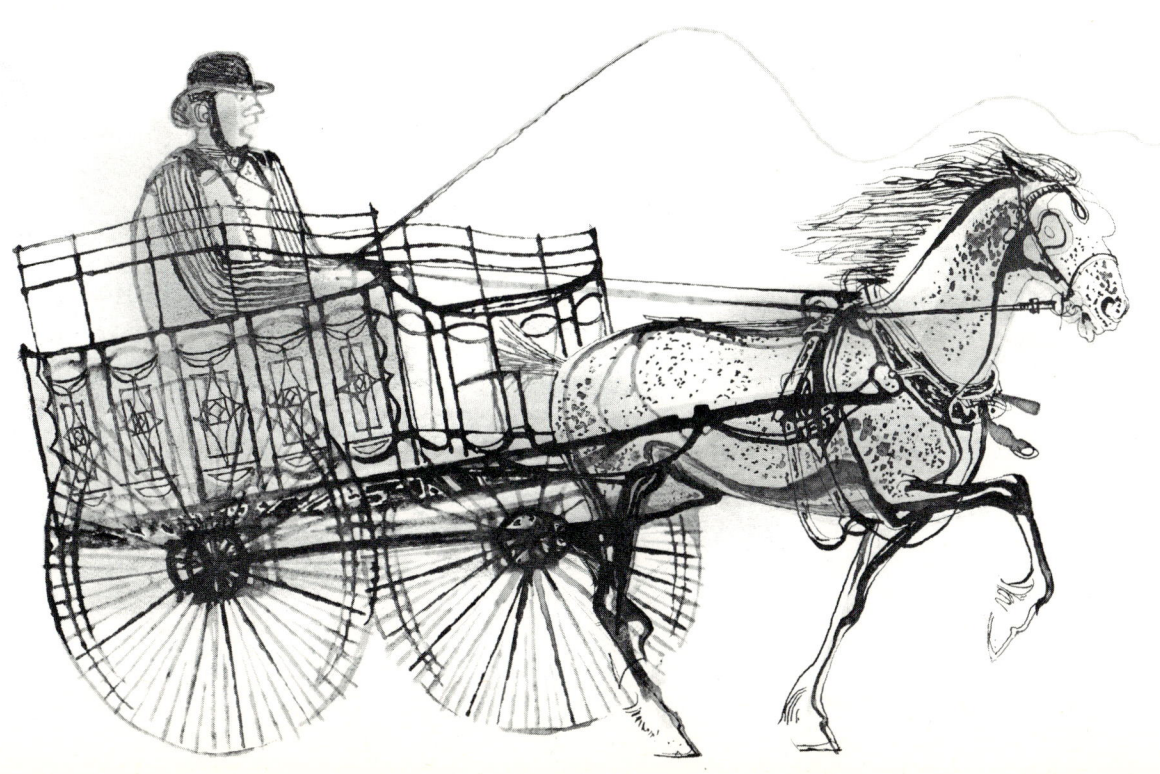

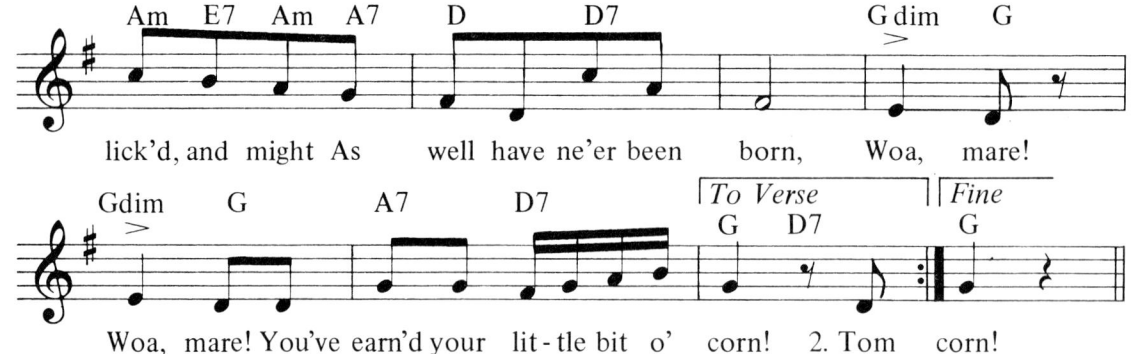

DOWN THE ROAD

1 Since first I copp'd a tidy lump o' swag
I've always kept a decent little nag;
But one as I shall sing about to you, now,
Was worth a million jimmies in a bag.
I match'd her 'gainst the best that could be found,
Four owners made a stake of sixty pound,
So the race was duly run,
And I'll tell you how I won
With brave Polly, my old pony, world renowned.

Down the road
Away went Polly,
With a step so jolly,
That I knew she'd win;
Down the road,
The pace was killing,
But the mare was willing
For a lightning spin;
All the rest were lick'd, and might
As well have ne'er been born,
Woa, mare! Woa, mare!
You've earn'd your little bit o' corn!

2 Tom Jones the butcher thought that form untrue!
　Says he 'Look here, I'll tell you what I'll do,
　My cob shall trot your mare again next Monday,
　And fifty more bright sov-rins I will blue;
　If you prove she can beat him once again,
　I'll never more in this world touch a rein!'
　Though I knew he'd got no chance,
　He insisted on the dance,
　So now I must tell you how we slew the slain.

　　Down the road
　　Away went Polly,
　　With a step so jolly,
　　That I knew she'd win;
　　Down the road,
　　The pace was killing,
　　But the mare was willing
　　For a lightning spin;
　　Jones's cob was lick'd, and might
　　As well have ne'er been born,
　　Woa, mare! Woa, mare!
　　You've earn'd your little bit o' corn!

3 Soon after that she reached the final goal,
　(I'd had the little wonder from a foal)
　And grief too keen to talk about was mine, when
　Poor Poll was carted off to fill a hole.
　My missus and the kids all went with me
　The last of poor pet pony Poll to see;
　And our neighbours shar'd the grief,
　That was felt beyond belief,
　When the little mare was buried. R.I.P.

　　Down the road
　　Away went Polly,
　　Not a face look'd jolly,
　　'Twould have seem'd a sin;
　　Down the road
　　The pace was killing,
　　But the dead mare willing
　　For the final spin;
　　Ev'rybody look'd so sad,
　　And I felt so forlorn,
　　Woa, mare! Woa, mare!
　　You've earn'd your little bit o' corn!

My London Country Lane

1. Now I have to live in London, bricks and mortar ev'rywhere,
   And there's miles of streets whichever way you turn,
   What with traffic and the crowdedness and smoke what's in the air,
   For a taste of country life I often yearn;
   So in the summer mornings from my domicile I roll,
   The moment that the sun shines on the pane,
   And although it's only makebelieve, I has a quiet stroll,
   Just a little country walk, down Drury Lane.

   Oh, I loves to take a ramble down my London country lane,
   And ev'ry time I has the chance I'm going there again;
   Tho' there ain't no ploughs and harrows,
   And the larks is mostly sparrers,
   Still, it's painted up and sez so – it's a real live lane!

2. Oh, I hate the roads and pavements, though I am a cockney chap,
   And I'm tired of the very name of 'street' –
   If at any time I cocks my eye upon a London map,
   I can feel the corns a-growing on my feet;
   But I'm fresh as any farmer when in Drury Lane I walk,
   And the piggies, sheep and rabbits I can see –
   Though the pretty baas are hanging in the butcher's with the pork,
   And the bunnies are as Ostend as can be.

   Oh, I loves to take a ramble down my London country lane,
   Where the nippers chuck things at you, and it isn't golden grain,
   Though the scarlet beans and marrows,
   Doesn't grow – they're all on barrows,
   Still, it's painted up and sez so – it's a real live lane!

3. When the London streets are baking, and there ain't a bit of breeze,
   You'll find the lane is quite a shady bower,
   You can see the corn a-standing in the fields beneath the trees –
   On the bags in which the baker sells the flour;
   You can hear the village natives using Middlesexy words
   To the waggoner what drives the brewer's dray,
   And you're almost sure to drop upon a 'downey' lot of birds,
   Though you very seldom comes across a jay.

Oh, I loves to take a ramble down my London country lane,
Where I meet the rustic maiden and I sing 'My pretty Jane';
Though I never twigs the squire
Nor observe the willage spire,
Still, it's painted up and sez so – it's a real live lane!

MY LONDON COUNTRY LANE

Words by Edgar Bateman. Music by Albert Perry

Now I have to live in London, bricks and mor-tar ev-'ry-where, And there's miles of streets which-ev-er way you turn, What with traf-fic and the crowd-ed-ness and smoke what's in the air, For a taste of coun-try life I of-ten yearn; So in the sum-mer morn-ings from my dom-i-cile I roll, The mo-ment that the sun shines on the pane, And al-though it's on-ly make-be-lieve, I has a qui-et stroll, Just a

Copyright by FRANCIS, DAY & HUNTER LTD., London.

E7 A7
lit - tle coun - try walk, down Dru - ry Lane. Oh, I
CHORUS
D
loves to take a ram - ble down my Lon - don coun - try lane, And
Daug D6 D7 G6 B♭7 A7
ev - 'ry time I has the chance I'm go - ing there a - gain; Tho' there
D Ddim D E7 A7
ain't no ploughs and har - rows, And the larks is most - ly spar - rers, Still, it's
D G E7 Em7 A7 D
paint - ed up and sez so, it's a real live lane!

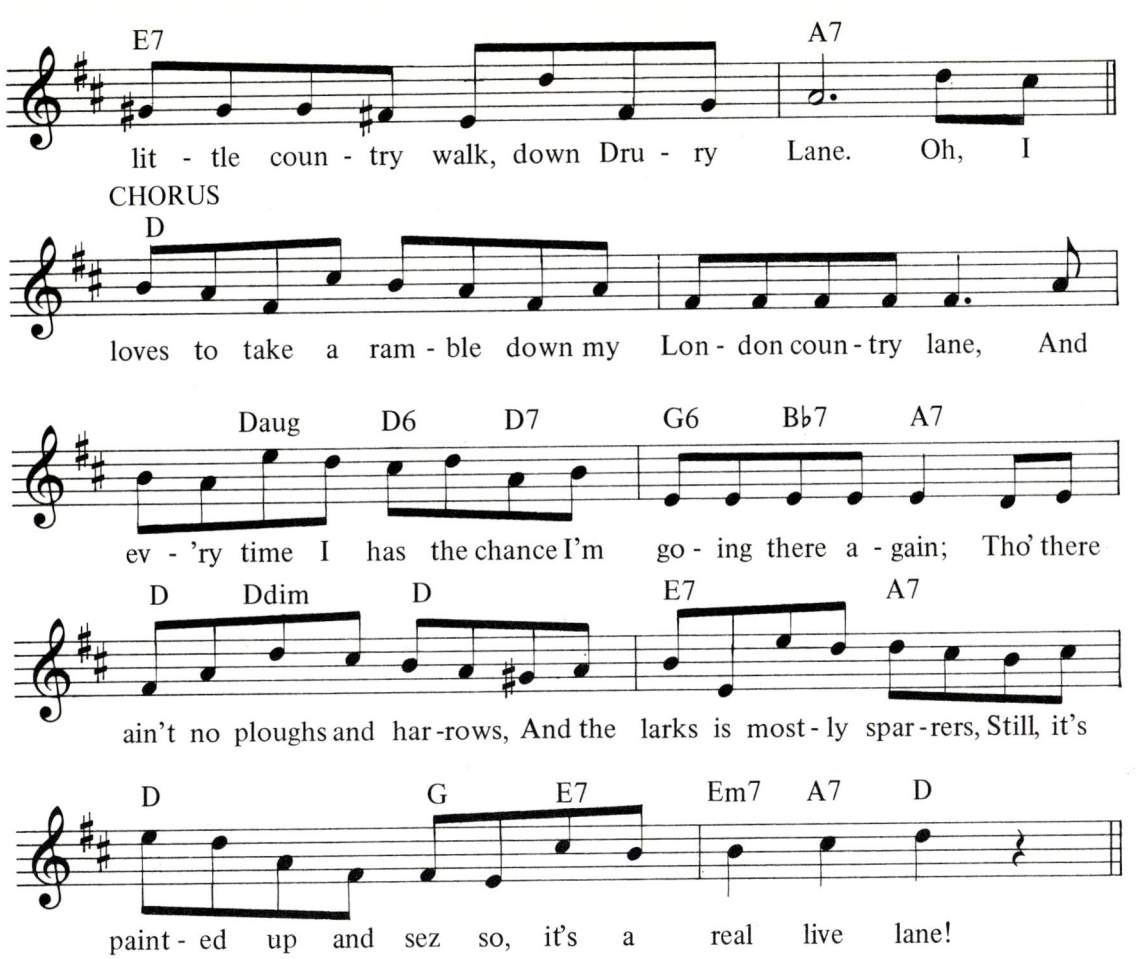

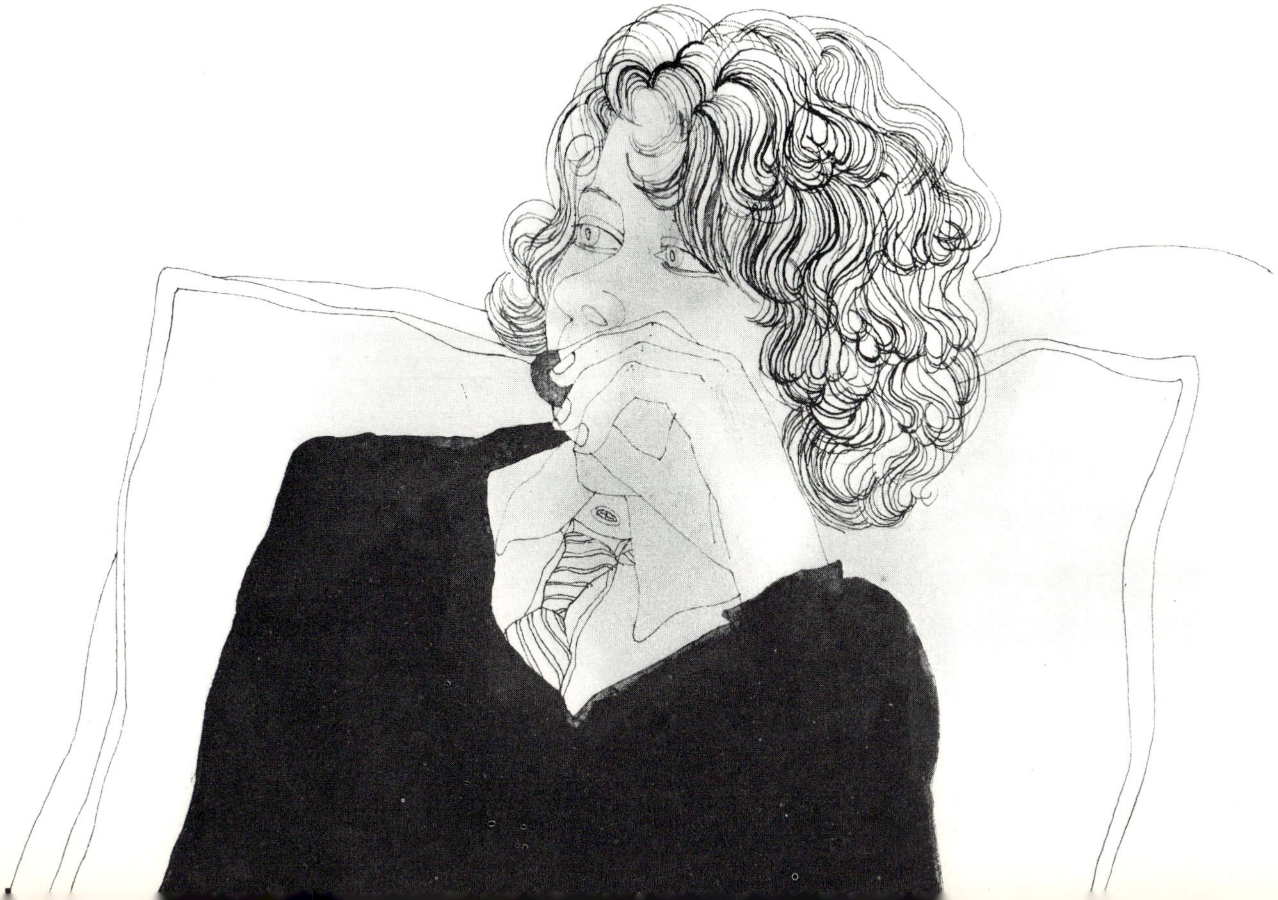

It's a Great Big Shame

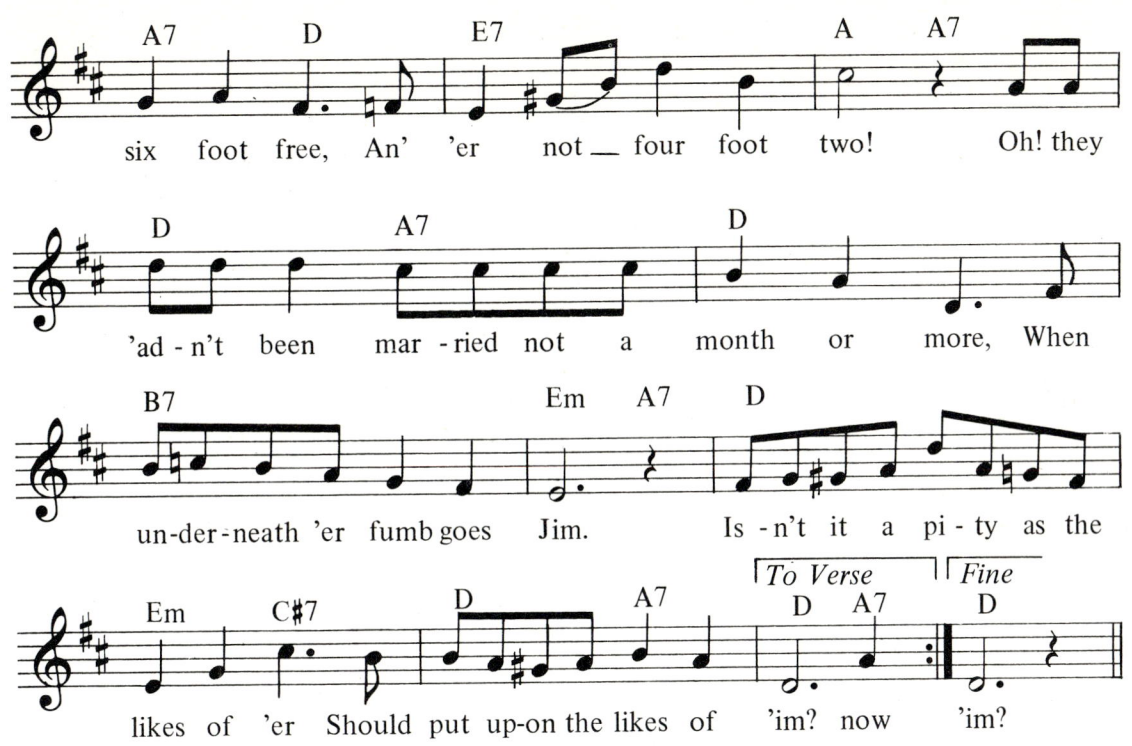

IT'S A GREAT BIG SHAME

1 I've lost my pal, 'e's the best in all the tahn,
But don't you fink 'im dead, becos 'e ain't
But since 'e's wed 'e 'as 'ad ter 'nuckle dahn
It's enufter wex the temper of a saint!
'E's a brewer's drayman, wiv a leg o'mutton fist,
An' as strong as a bullick or an 'orse,
Yet in 'er 'ands 'e's like a little kid –
Oh! I wish as I could get 'im a divorce.

> *It's a great big shame, an' if she belong'd ter me*
> *I'd let 'er know who's who,*
> *Naggin' at a feller wot is six foot free,*
> *An' 'er not four foot two!*
> *Oh! they 'adn't been married not a month or more,*
> *When underneath 'er fumb goes Jim.*
> *Isn't it a pity as the likes of 'er*
> *Should put upon the likes of 'im?*

2   Now Jim was class 'e could sing a decent song,
    And at scrappin' 'e 'ad won some great renown;
    It took two coppers for ter make 'im move along,
    And an-nuvver six to 'old the feller dahn.
    But today when I axes would 'e come an' 'ave some beer,
    To the doorstep on tiptoe 'e arrives
    'I daren't,' says 'e. 'Don't shout, cos she'll 'ear –
    I've got ter clean the windows an' the knives.'

3   On a Sunday morn, wiv a dozen pals or more,
    'E'd play at pitch and toss along the Lea;
    But now she bullies 'im a scrubbin' 'o the floor
    Such a change, well, I never did see.
    Wiv a apron on 'im, I twigged 'im, on 'is knees
    A rubbin' up the old 'arfstone;
    Wot wiv emptyin' the ashes and a shellin' o' the peas,
    I'm blowed if 'e can call 'isself 'is own!

Wot's the Good of Hanyfink! Why! Nuffink!

Copyright by REYNOLDS MUSIC, London. All Rights Reserved.

WOT'S THE GOOD OF HANYFINK! WHY! NUFFINK!

1. This world's a disappointment, yuss!
   On that score my mind's made up;
   The chances is unequal quite,
   The few I've had I've weigh'd up,
   An' arter lots of thinkin',
   'Ave come to this conclusion,
   That hev'ryfink in life is but
   A snare an' a delusion.

   Wot's the good of tryin' to hearn a livin' now-a-days?
   Wot's the good of honesty when 'umbug only pays?
   Wot's the good of slavin' o' a ravin' about savin'?
   Wot's the good of hanyfink? Why! . . . Nuffink!

35

2   They say wiv my appearance that
    I never takes no trouble,
    That on my chin there allus is
    At least a two days' stubble.
    I used ter shave each mornin' when
    A razor I could borrer,
    But chucked it cos it only meant
    A scrape agin to-morrer!

Wot's the good of tryin to hearn a livin' now-a-days?
Wot's the good of honesty when 'umbug only pays?
Wot's the good of shavin'? costs a penny–worth while savin'
Wot's the good of hanyfink? Why! . . . Nuffink!

3   I'ave thought as I'd marry 'cos
    I'm so domesticated,
    But women's sich a funny lot
    The sex is over-rated!
    Suppose I settled down in life,
    I'd 'ave ter find a missus,
    Then fancy me a comin' 'ome
    Ter bread an' cheese an' kisses!

Wot's the good of tryin' to hearn a livin' now-a-days?
Wot's the good of honesty when 'umbug only pays?
Wot's the good of spoonin'? might as well take on balloonin'
Wot's the good of hanyfink? Why! . . . Nuffink!

4   Now when I goes ter bed at night,
    I seldom takes my boots off,
    Cos if I gits a job – at five
    I nearly allus scoots off!
    An' then I as ter 'unt about,
    There's sich a job ter find 'em
    An' so I keeps 'em on, an' pon
    My word I never mind 'em!

Wot's the good of tryin' to hearn a livin' now-a-days?
Wot's the good of honesty when 'umbug only pays?
Wot's the good of messin' about dressin'? 'tain't no blessin'
Wot's the good of hanyfink? Why! . . . Nuffink!

When the Old Dun Cow Caught Fire

1   Some pals and I in a public house
    Were playing dominoes last night,
    When all of a sudden in the potman runs
    With a face just like a kite.
    'What's up?' said Jones. 'Why you silly old fool
    Have you seen old Aunt Maria?'
    'Aunt be blowed,' then the potman cried,
    'The blooming pub's on fire.'
    'On fire!' said Brown, 'What a bit of luck!
    Come along with me,' shouts he.
    'Down in the cellar, if the fire ain't there,
    We'll have a fair old spree.'
    So we all goes down 'long with good old Brown,
    Booze we couldn't miss,
    We hadn't been ten minutes there,
    When I was just like this.

   *And there was Brown, upside down,
   Licking up the whisky off the floor,
   'Booze! booze! booze!' then the firemen cried,
   As they got knocking down the door.
   'Don't let 'em in till it's all mopped up,'
   Some-one said to Mackintyre,
   So we all got blue blind, paralytic drunk
   When the Old Dun Cow caught fire.*

2   Old Johnson flew to a port wine tub,
    And he gave it just a few hard knocks,
    He then starts taking off his pantaloons!
    Ditto his boots and socks.
    'Hold hard,' said Snooks, 'if you want to wash your feet
    There's a barrel full of four ale here.
    Don't put your trotters in the port wine Jack
    When there's some old style beer.'
    Just then there was such a dreadful crash
    Half the blooming roof gave way,
    We got drownded with a fireman's hose,
    But still we were all gay;

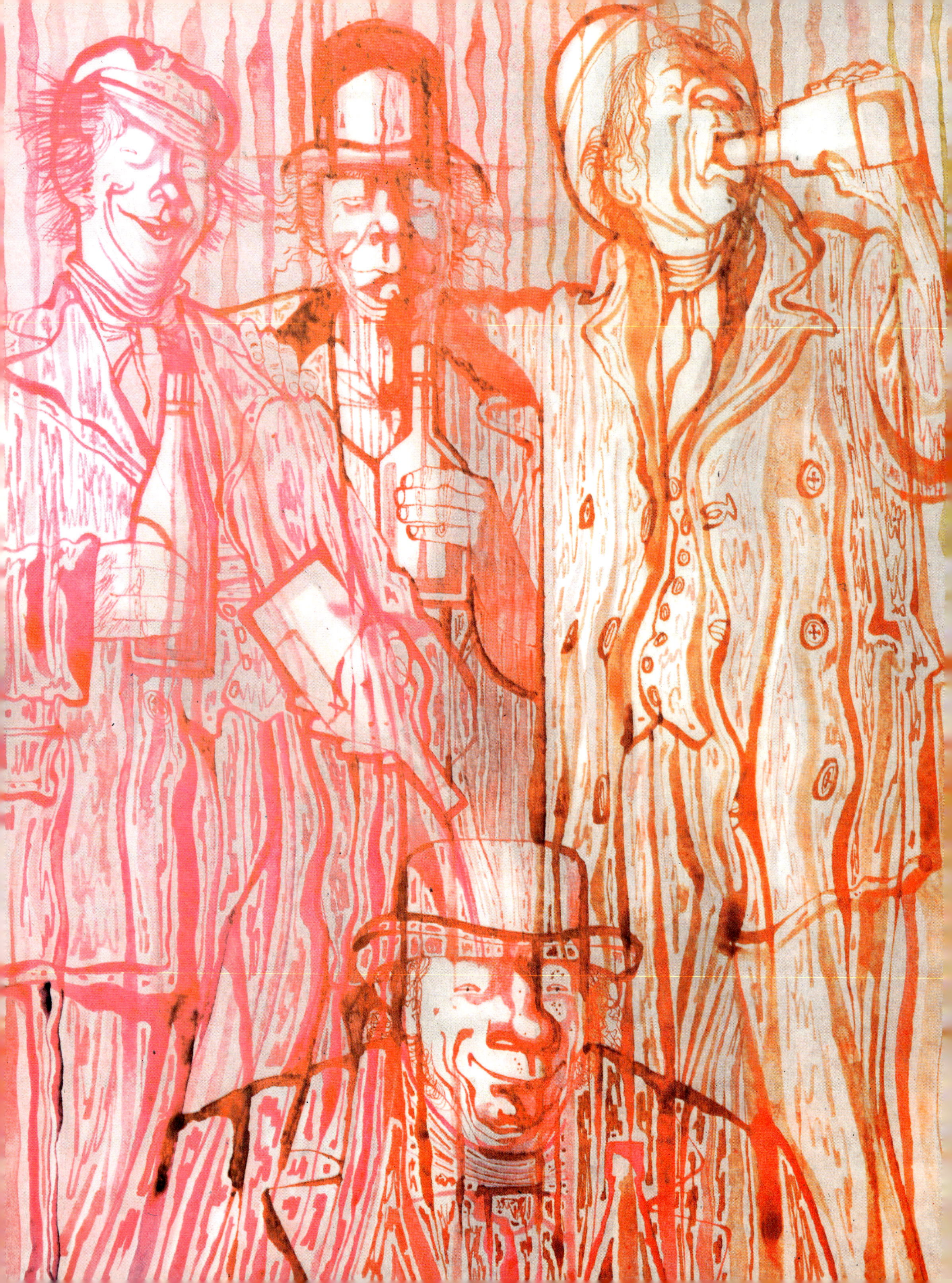

    For we found some sacks, and some old tin tacks
Shoved ourselves inside,
We all got drinking good old scotch,
Till we got bleary eye'd.

3   We got so drunk that we did not know
The blooming cellar had caught fire,
Poor old Jones had the DT's bad
And wanted to retire.
'There's "old Nick",' said another poor chap,
'And he's poking up the blooming fire.'
'That's no bogy, it's a fireman Tom
At least,' said Mackintyre.
'Let's get out,' said a blind-eye'd boy,
'It's getting rather hot down here.'
'Don't be a fool,' said a boozy bloke,
'We haven't drunk the beer.'
So we filled our hats, and we drank like cats
'Midst the flames and smoke,
I had to take my trousers off
I thought that I should croak.

4   At last the firemen got inside
And found us all dead drunk,
But like true heroes there they stood
They did not do a bunk.
They saw the booze upon the floor
And gave a sudden yell
They took their helmets off and then
Upon their knees they fell.
'At last! at last!' the firemen cried,
'At last we know the news.'
'Come on, come on,' us lads all cried
'Come on and have a booze.'

WHEN THE OLD DUN COW CAUGHT FIRE

Words and music by Harry Wincott

Moderato

Some pals and I in a pub-lic house Were play-ing dom-in-oes last night, When all of a sud-den in the pot-man runs With a face just like a kite. 'What's up?' said Jones. 'Why you sil-ly old fool Have you seen old Aunt Ma-ria?' 'Aunt be blowed,' then the pot-man cried, 'The bloom-ing pub's on fire.' 'On fire!' said Brown, 'What a bit o' luck! Come a-long with me,' shouts he. 'Down in the cel-lar, if the fire ain't there, We'll have a fair old spree.' So we

Copyright by REEDER & WALSH.

Dm Gm
all goes down 'long with good old Brown, Booze we could - n't
Dm A7 Dm Gm6
miss, We had - n't been ten min - utes there, When
A7 Dm A7 CHORUS Dm
I was just like this. And there was Brown, up - side down,
B♭ A Gm C7
Lick-ing up the whis-ky off the floor, 'Booze! booze! booze!' then the
F C G7 C A7
fire - men cried, As they got knock - ing down the door.
Dm B♭ F B♭
'Don't let 'em in till it's all mopp'd up,' Some-one said to Mack-in-
A7 Dm A7 Dm
tyre, So we all got blue blind, par - a - ly - tic drunk When the
A7 1 Dm 2 Dm
Old Dun Cow caught fire And fire

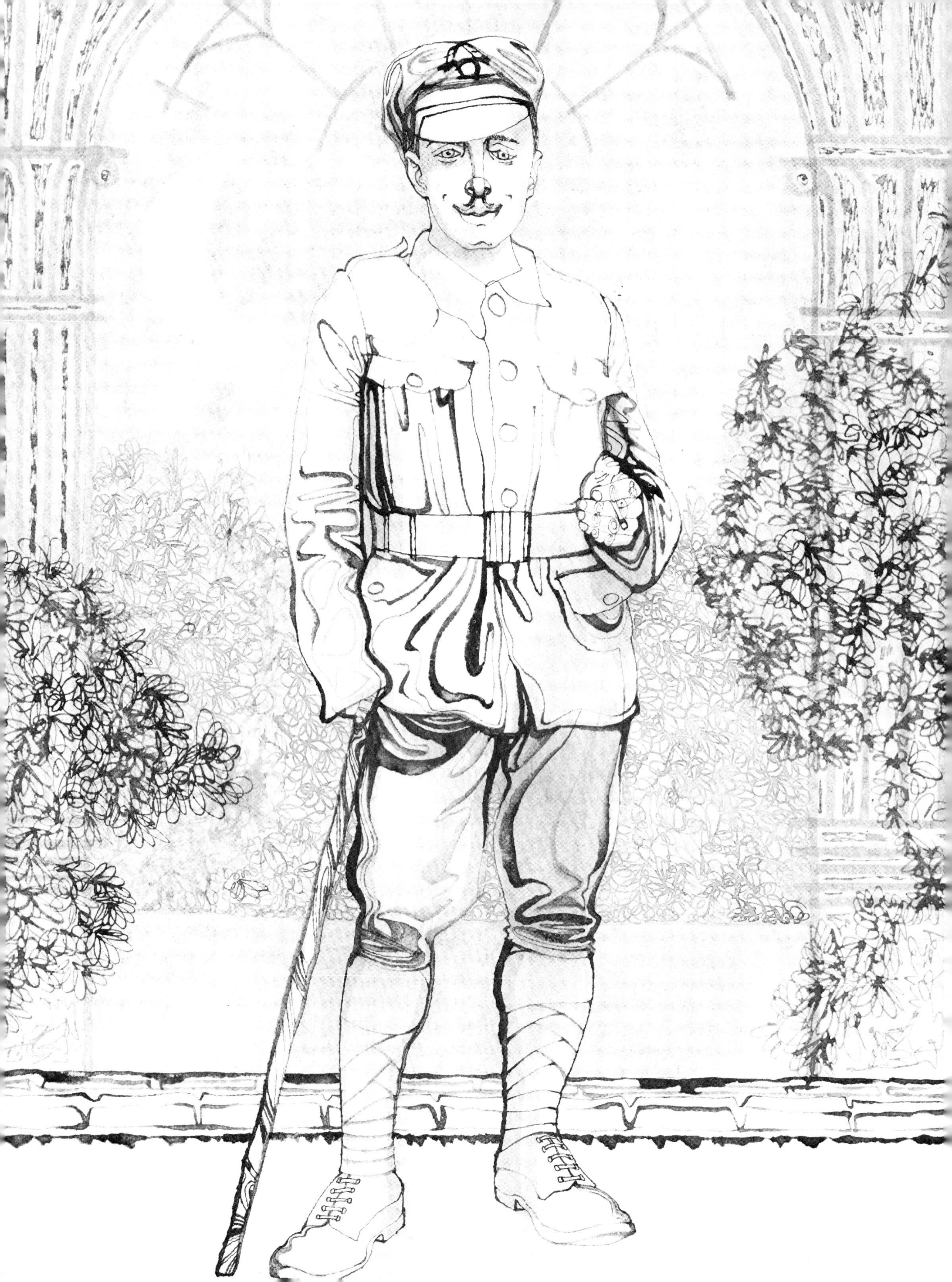

The D.C.M.

1 You never know what you can do till you're put to the test,
If you've got lots of pluck, and just a little luck,
You keep on persevering and you leave behind the rest,
Then you'll have medals like these I've not got on my chest.
They're all through doing deeds of bravery.
If you want an example look at me.

First I went and won the 'D.C.M.',
Then I went and won the 'D.S.O.',
And then I went and won the 'A.B.C.', the 'D.F.G.',
The 'H.I.J.K.L.M.N.O.P.' And then I went and won the 'R.S.T.'
My word how I fought and bled,
Ev'ry word I say is true,
I won the 'U.V.W.'
And now I've been and won the 'X.Y.Z.'

2 I ne'er shall forget the time when I was out in Timbuctoo,
When I was there you see, they called me Timbucthree,
They soon found out I was victorious for my deeds of daring do,
I even won first prize I did for drinking Roderick Dew.
The things I won would nearly fill a sack,
I'd such a lot I sent half of them back.

SPOKEN: Guns on shoulders put, two's into four get.
　　　　 Rifles sloped, bullets put in. BANG! BANG!
　　　　　 War's all over.

First I went and won the 'D.C.M.',
Then I went and won the 'D.S.O.',
Then I went and won the 'A.B.C.', the 'D.E.F.G.',
The 'H.I.J.K.L.M.N.O.P.' And then I went and won the 'R.S.T.',
And the colonel, he said 'Joe,
We've no whisky, rum or gin, and the beer is all done in,
So you'd better have an "O.X.O."'

THE D.C.M.

Allegretto

Collected by Charles Keeping

You ne-ver know what you can do till you're put to the test, If you've got lots of pluck, and just a lit-tle luck, You keep on per-se-ver-ing and you leave be-hind the rest, Then you'll have med-als like these I've not got on my chest. *Slower* They're all through do-ing deeds of bra-ver-y. If you want an ex-am-ple look at me. First I *a tempo* went and won the 'D. C. M.', Then I went and won the 'D. S. O.', And then I went and

This arrangement © 1975 by BRITISH AND CONTINENTAL MUSIC AGENCIES LTD.

won the 'A. B. C., the 'D. F. G., The 'H. I. J. K. L. M. N. O. P.' And then I went and won the 'R. S. T.' My word how I fought and bled, Ev'ry word I say is true, I won the 'U V. dou-ble U' And now I've been and won the 'X. Y. Z.'

Fine.

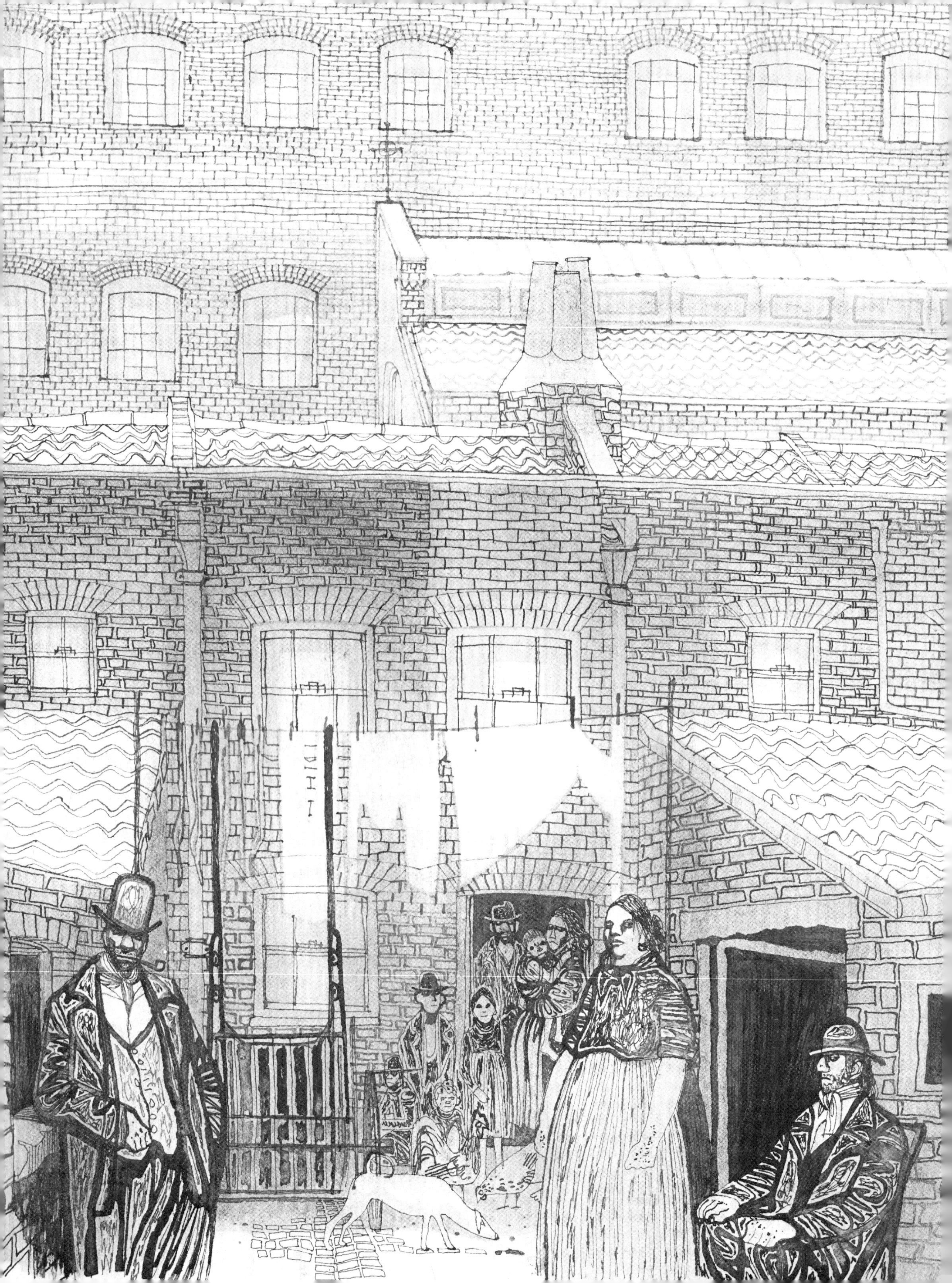

If It Wasn't For the 'Ouses In Between

1. If you saw my little backyard, 'Wot a pretty spot' you'd cry,
   It's a picture on a sunny summer day;
   Wiv the turnip-tops and cabbages wot peoples doesn't buy
   I makes it on a Sunday look all gay.
   The neighbours finks I grow 'em and you'd fancy you're in Kent,
   Or at Epsom if you gaze into the mews;
   It's a wonder as the landlord doesn't want to raise the rent
   Because we've got such nobby distant views.

   Oh! it really is a werry pretty garden,
   And Chingford to the eastward could be seen;
   Wiv a ladder and some glasses,
   You could see to 'Ackney Marshes,
   If it wasn't for the 'ouses in between.

2. We're as countrified as can be wiv a clothes-prop for a tree,
   The tubstool makes a rustic little stile;
   Ev'ry time the blooming clock strikes there's a cuckoo sings to me,
   And I've painted up 'To Leather Lane a mile'.
   Wiv tomatoes and wiv radishes wot 'adn't any sale,
   The backyard looks a puffick mass of bloom,
   And I've made a little beehive wiv some beetles in a pail,
   And a pitchfork wiv the handle of a broom.

   Oh! it really is a werry pretty garden,
   And Rye 'Ouse from the cockloft could be seen;
   Where the chickweed man undresses,
   To bathe 'mong the water cresses,
   If it wasn't for the 'ouses in between.

3. There's the bunny shares 'is egg-box wiv the cross-eyed cock and hen,
   Though they 'as got the pip, and him the morf;
   In a dog's 'ouse on the line-post there was pigeons nine or ten,
   Till someone took a brick and knock'd it off.
   The dustcart, though it seldom comes, is just like 'arvest 'ome.
   And we mean to rig a dairy up some'ow,
   Put the donkey in the wash-house wiv some imitation 'orns,
   For we're teaching 'im to moo just like a kah.

Oh! it really is a werry pretty garden,
'En-don to the westward could be seen;
And by clinging to the chimbley,
You could see across to Wembley,
If it wasn't for the 'ouses in between.

4 Though the gas-works isn't wi-lets, they improve the rural scene
For mountains they would very nicely pass;
There's the mushrooms in the dust-hole with the cowcumbers so green
It only wants a bit o' 'ot-'ouse glass.
I wears this milk-man's night shirt, and I sits outside all day,
Like the ploughboy cove what's mizzled o'er the Lea;
And when I goes indoors at night they dunno what I say,
Cause my language gets as yokel as can be.

Oh! it really is a werry pretty garden,
And soapworks from the 'ouse tops could be seen;
If I got a rope and pulley,
I'd enjoy the breeze more fully,
If it wasn't for the 'ouses in between.

IF IT WASN'T FOR THE 'OUSES IN BETWEEN

Words by Edgar Bateman. Music by George le Brunn

If you saw my little back-yard, 'Wot a pret-ty spot' you'd cry, It's a pic-ture on a sun-ny sum-mer day; Wiv the tur-nip tops and cab-ba-ges wot peo-ples does-n't buy I makes it on a Sun-day look all

Copyright by FRANCIS, DAY & HUNTER., London.

gay. The ___ neigh-bours finks I grow 'em and you'd fan-cy you're in Kent, Or at Ep-som if you gaze in-to the mews; It's a won-der as the land-lord does-n't want to raise the rent Be-cause we've got such nob-by dis-tant views.

CHORUS

Oh! it real-ly is a wer-ry pret-ty gar-den, And Chingford to the east-ward could be seen; Wiv a lad-der and some glass-es, You could see to 'Ack-ney Marsh-es, If it was-n't for the 'ous-es in be-tween We're as tween

In the Shade of the Old Apple Tree

Valse moderato

Words by Harry H. Williams. Music by Egbert van Alstyne

In the shade of the old ap-ple tree,____ When the love in your eyes I could see.____ When the voice that I heard, like the song of the bird, Seem'd to whis-per sweet mus-ic to me.____ I could hear the dull buzz of the bee,____ In the blos-soms as you said to me,____ 'With a heart that is true I'll be wait-ing for you, In the shade of the old ap-ple tree.'____ In the tree.'____

Copyright by FRANCIS, DAY & HUNTER LTD., London.

IN THE SHADE OF THE OLD APPLE TREE

1 The oriole with joy was sweetly singing,
  The little brook was babbling forth its tune;
  The village bells at noon were gaily ringing,
  The world seem'd brighter than a harvest moon.
  For there within my arms I gently press'd you,
  And flushing red, you slowly turned away.
  I can't forget the way I once caressed you,
  I can't forget that bygone happy day.

2 In the shade of the old apple tree,
  When the love in your eyes I could see.
  When the voice that I heard, like the song of the bird,
  Seem'd to whisper sweet music to me.
  I could hear the dull buzz of the bee,
  In the blossoms as you said to me,
  'With a heart that is true
  I'll be waiting for you,
  In the shade of the old apple tree.'

(PARODY)

Oh an Englishman, a Frenchman and a Hebrew
Were sentenced to be hung one summer's day;
They asked the Frenchman what tree he'd like to die on,
And he chose the pear tree straight away;
Oh they hung him on the pear tree and he died happily.
The Englishman said, 'Any bloody tree will do for me.'
So on the old apple tree they put his lights out
When suddenly a word came from the Jew.

'Hang me please on the gooseberry tree.
Vill you do this kind favour for me?
It's my dying request – it's the tree I love best –
Hang me please on the gooseberry tree.'
Oh the judge said, 'You really must know,
That a gooseberry tree does not grow.'
I'm in no hurry,' said Moses,
'I vill vait till it grows, to the size of
The old apple tree.'

They're Moving Father's Grave to Build a Sewer

Collected by Charles Keeping

Oh, they're mov-ing fath-er's grave to build a sew-er, _____ They're mov-ing it re-gard-less of ex-pense. They're shift-ing his re-mains, to put in five-inch drains, To irr-i-gate some posh bloke's res-id-ence. Now in his life-time fath-er nev-er was a quitt-er, And I'm sure that he won't be a quitt-er now, For when that job's com-plete, he'll haunt that privv-y seat, And he'll on-ly let them sit when he'll a-llow. Oh,

This arrangement © 1975 by BRITISH AND CONTINENTAL MUSIC AGENCIES LTD.

THEY'RE MOVING FATHER'S GRAVE TO BUILD A SEWER

Oh, they're moving father's grave to build a sewer,
They're moving it regardless of expense.
They're shifting his remains, to put in five-inch drains,
To irrigate some posh bloke's residence.
Now in his lifetime father never was a quitter,
And I'm sure that he won't be a quitter now,
For when that job's complete, he'll haunt that privvy seat,
And he'll only let them sit when he'll allow.
Oh, won't there be some bleeding consternation,
And won't those city chappies rant and rave,
Which is no more than they deserve,
To have the bloody nerve,
To muck about with a British workman's grave.

Wot Cher!

1. Last week down our alley come a toff,
   Nice old geezer with a nasty cough,
   Sees my missus, takes 'is topper off
   In a very gentlemanly way!
   'Ma'am,' says he, 'I 'ave some news to tell,
   Your rich uncle Tom of Camberwell,
   Popped off recent, which it ain't a sell,
   Leaving you 'is little Donkey Shay.'

   > 'Wot cher!' all the neighbours cried,
   > 'Who're yer goin' to meet, Bill?
   > Have yer bought the street, Bill?'
   > Laugh! I thought I should 'ave died,
   > Knock'd 'em in the Old Kent Road!

2. Some says nasty things about the moke,
   One cove thinks 'is leg is really broke,
   That's 'is envy, cos we're carriage folk,
   Like the toffs as rides in Rotten Row!
   Straight! it woke the alley up a bit,
   Thought our lodger would 'ave 'ad a fit,
   When my missus, who's a real wit,
   Says 'I 'ates a Bus because it's low!'

3. When we starts the blessed donkey stops,
   He won't move, so out I quickly 'ops,
   Pals start whackin' him, when down he drops,
   Someone says he wasn't made to go.
   Lor it might 'ave been a four in 'and,
   My old Dutch knows 'ow to do the grand,
   First she bows, and then she waves 'er 'and,
   Calling out, 'We're goin' for a blow!'

4. Ev'ry evenin' on the stroke of five,
   Me and missus takes a little drive,
   You'd say, 'Wonderful they're still alive,'
   If you saw that little donkey go.
   I soon showed him that 'e'd have to do,
   Just whatever he was wanted to,
   Still I shan't forget that rowdy crew,
   'Ollerin' 'Woa! steady! Neddy Woa!'

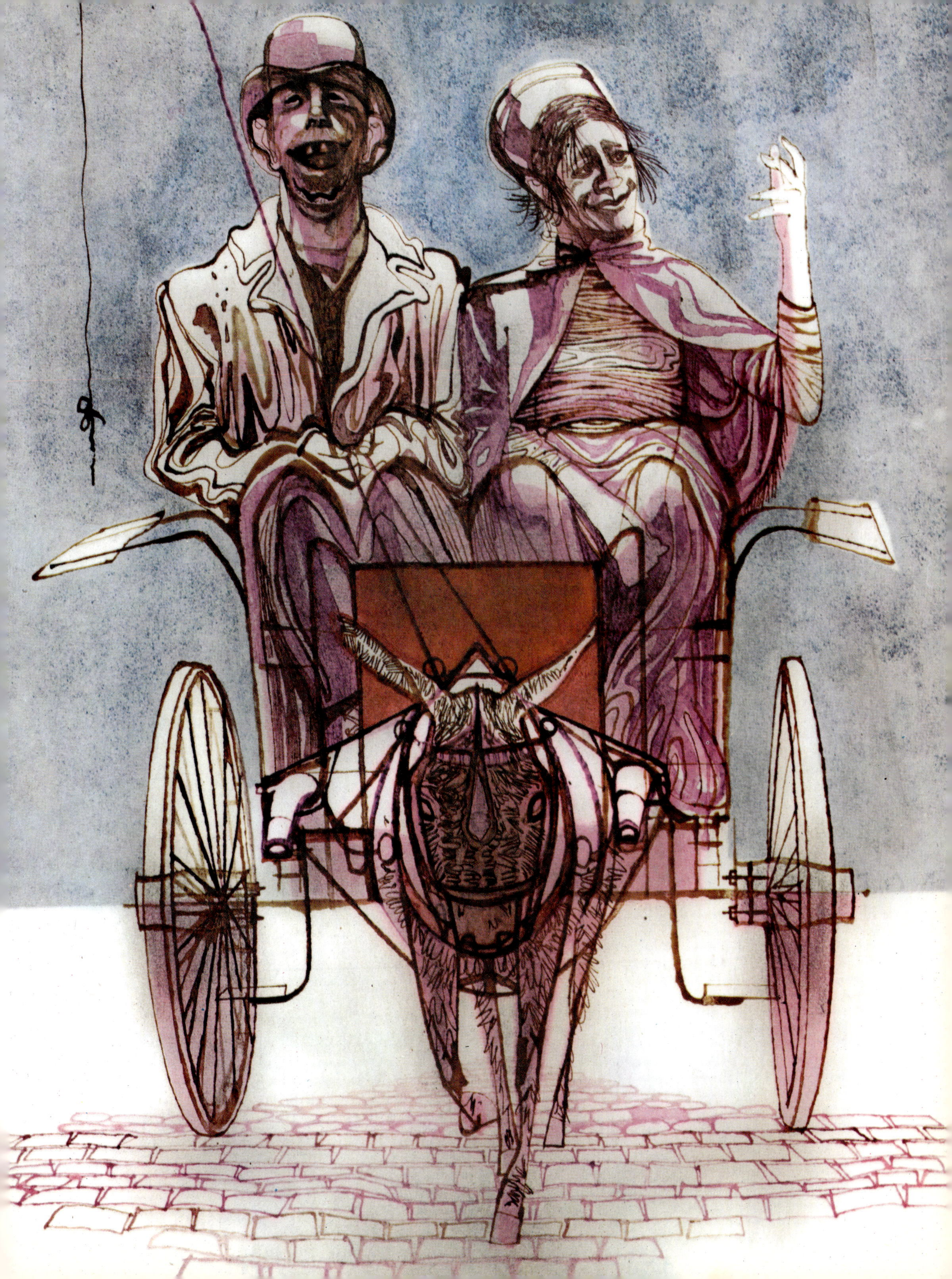

WOT CHER!

Words by Albert Chevalier. Music by Charles Ingle.

VERSE

Last week down our all-ey come a toff,
Nice old gee-zer with a nas-ty cough, Sees my miss-us, takes 'is top-per off In a ver-y gen-tle-man-ly way! 'Ma'am,' says he, 'I 'ave some news to tell, Your rich un-cle Tom of Cam-ber-well, Popped off re-cent, which it ain't a sell, Leav-ing you 'is lit-tle Donk-ey Shay.'

CHORUS

'Wot cher!' all the neigh-bours cried, 'Who're yer goin' to meet, Bill?

Copyright by REYNOLDS MUSIC, London.

Have yer bought the street, Bill?' Laugh! I thought I should 'ave died, Knock'd 'em in the Old Kent Road! Road!

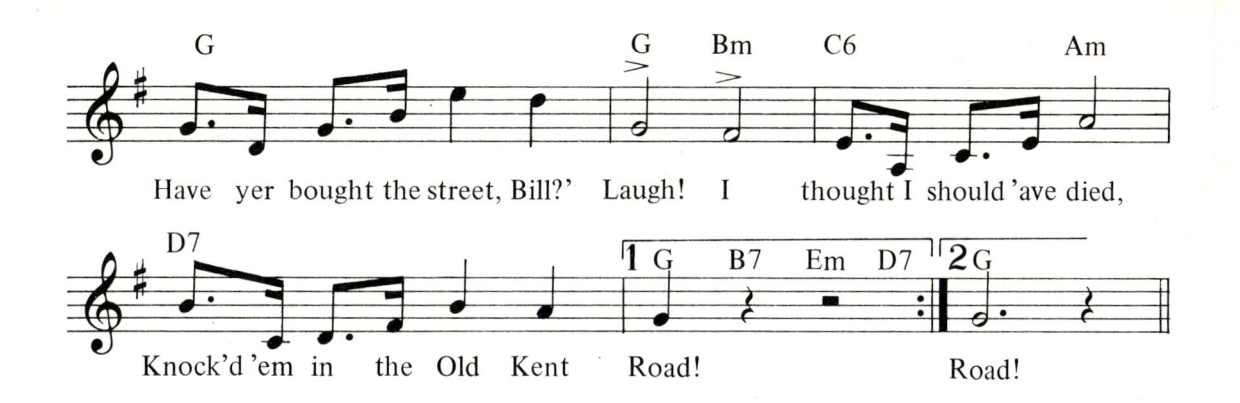

Where Did You Get That Hat?

Moderato **VERSE**

Words and music by Charles Rolmas

Now how I came to get this hat, 'tis ve-ry strange and fun-ny, Grand-fa-ther died and left to me his pro-per-ty and mon-ey; And when the will it was read out, they told me straight and flat, If I would have his mon-ey I must al-ways wear his hat!

CHORUS

'Where did you get that hat? Where did you get that tile? Is-n't it a nob-by one, and just the pro-per style? I should like to have one just the same as that!' Wher-e'er I go they shout 'Hel-lo! Where

(handwritten annotations: Arms on hips, legs apart / Tambourine / Arms out in front - palms up / All point / Arms on hips, legs apart / wave in the air)

Copyright by FRANCIS, DAY & HUNTER., London.

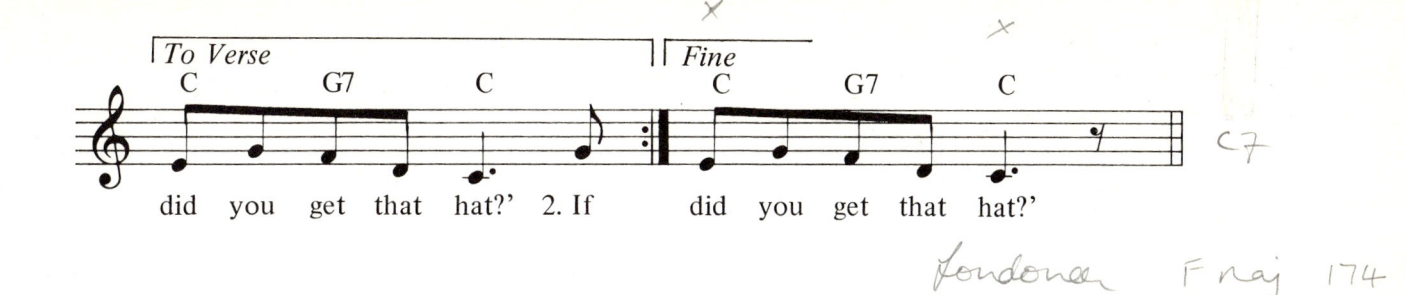

WHERE DID YOU GET THAT HAT?

1. Now how I came to get this hat, 'tis very strange and funny,
   Grandfather died and left to me his property and money;
   And when the will it was read out, they told me straight and flat,
   If I would have his money I must always wear his hat!

   SPOKEN: And everywhere I go, everyone shouts after me:

   'Where did you get that hat?
   Where did you get that tile?
   Isn't it a nobby one, and just the proper style?
   I should like to have one just the same as that!'
   Where'er I go they shout 'Hello! Where did you get that hat?'

2. If I go to the op'ra house, in the op'ra season,
   There's someone sure to shout at me without the slightest reason.
   If I go to a concert hall to have a jolly spree,
   There's someone in the party who is sure to shout at me:

3. At twenty-one I thought I would to my sweetheart get married,
   The people in the neighbourhood had said too long we'd tarried.
   So off to church we went right quick, determined to get wed;
   I had not long been in there, when the parson to me said:

4. I once tried hard to be MP but failed to get elected,
   Upon a tub I stood, round which a thousand folks collected;
   And I had dodged the eggs and bricks (which was no easy task),
   When one man cried, 'A question I the candidate would ask!'

   SPOKEN: I told him that I was ready to reply to any question that could be put to me. The man said: 'Thousands of British working people are anxiously awaiting enlightenment on the subject on which I am about to address you. It is a question of national importance, in fact; THE great problem of the day – and that is, Sir:

5 When Colonel South, the millionaire, gave his last garden party
I was amongst the guests who had a welcome true and hearty;
The Prince of Wales was also there, and my heart jumped with glee,
When I was told the Prince would like to have a word with me.

SPOKEN: I was immediately presented to His Royal Highness, who immediately exclaimed:

They're All Very Fine and Large

1. To be too modest nowadays,
Is not a thing that pays,
It's best to shout what you've to sell,
In these advertising days.
I say this song is something great,
To ventilate our wrongs,
But as for that, you all well know,
That nearly all my songs:

   They're all very fine and large!
   They're sound and fat and prime,
   If you think you can beat 'em,
   It will take you all your time.
   They're the widest in creation,
   And I make no extra charge,
   Who'll have a chance for a dozen or two,
   They're all very fine and large!

2. To the ladies I must dedicate,
At least one special verse,
We court, we love, we marry them,
Don't laugh, you might do worse.
And oh! those tasty, dressy ones,
Who pass you with a wink,
And always know your Christian name,
Do I like 'em? Well, I think:

3. Our policemen are a credit to
The land that gave 'em birth,
They're the pluckiest set of fellows,
You'll find upon the earth.
At the Crystal Palace, once a year,
On revelry they meet,
Who'll take a dozen tickets now
To see the p'licemen's fete?

4. I once rode in an omnibus,
And was so upset to find,
My fare it came to fourpence,
And I'd left my purse behind.
The conductor said, 'Look here, young chap,
This game won't do for me,
I'm going to take it out in kicks,'
And he only gave me three. But,

5. I thought I'd go to Margate once,
For rest and change of air,
But, oh! I lost some pounds of flesh,
The few days I was there.
I couldn't get a wink of sleep,
I shan't forget that bed,
The landlady said 'Do you like the rooms?'
I paid my bill, and said:

THEY'RE ALL VERY FINE AND LARGE

Moderato
Words and music by Frederick Bowyer

To — be too mod-est now-a-days, Is — not a thing that pays, It's best to shout what you've to sell, In these ad-ver-tis-ing days. I say this song is some-thing great, To ven-ti-late our wrongs, But as for that, you all well know, That near-ly all my songs —

CHORUS

They're all ve-ry fine and large! They're sound and fat and prime, If you think you can beat 'em, It will take you all your time. They're the

Copyright by FRANCIS, DAY & HUNTER LTD., London.

widest in creation, And I make no extra charge, Who'll have a chance for a dozen or two, They're all very fine and large! 2. To__ large!__

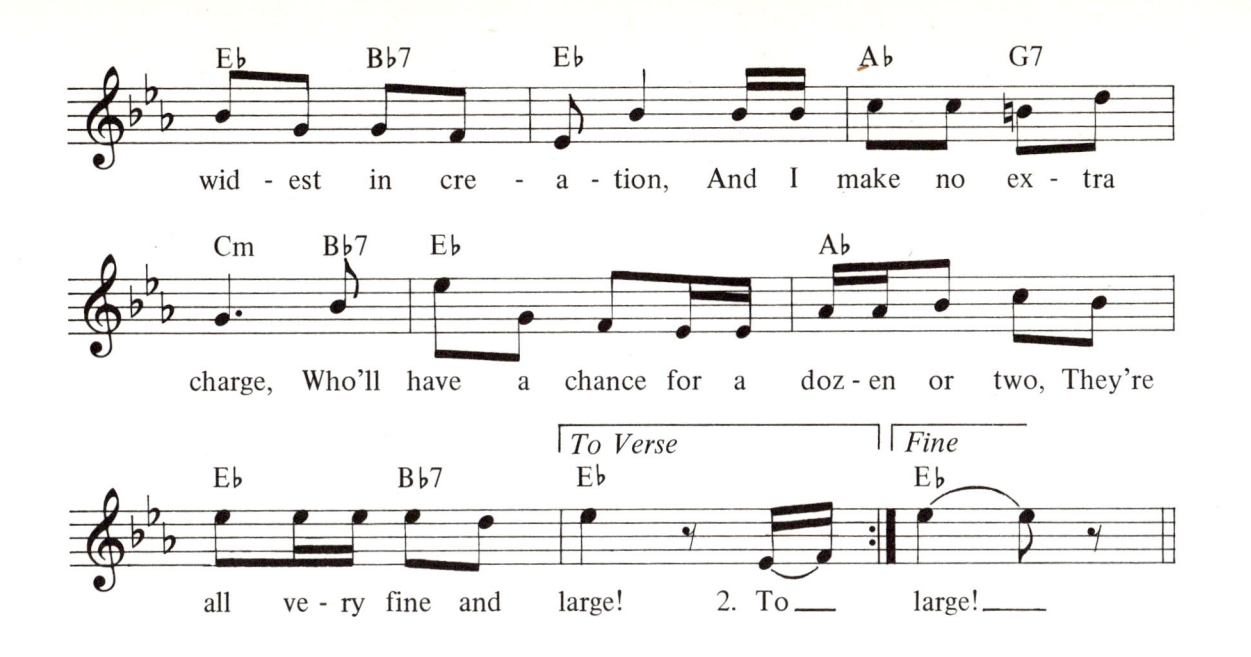

On Monday I Never Go to Work

Collected by Charles Keeping

On Mon-day I ne-ver go to work, On Tues-day I stay at home, On Wednes-day I don't feel in-clined, Work's the last thing on my mind. Thurs-day, half hol-i-day, And Fri-day I de-test; Too late to make a start on Sat-ur-day, And Sun-day is my day of rest. I don't know no one what don't want no nine-inch nails, I don't know no one what don't want no nine-inch nails, I know the King, I

This arrangement © 1975 by BRITISH AND CONTINENTAL MUSIC AGENCIES LTD.

ON MONDAY I NEVER GO TO WORK

1. On Monday I never go to work,
   On Tuesday I stay at home,
   On Wednesday I don't feel inclined,
   Work's the last thing on my mind.
   Thursday, half holiday,
   And Friday I detest;
   Too late to make a start on Saturday,
   And Sunday is my day of rest.

2. I don't know no one what don't want no nine-inch nails,
   I don't know no one what don't want no nine-inch nails,
   I know the King, I know the Queen, I know the Prince of Wales,
   All pubs,
   But I don't know no one what don't want no nine-inch nails.

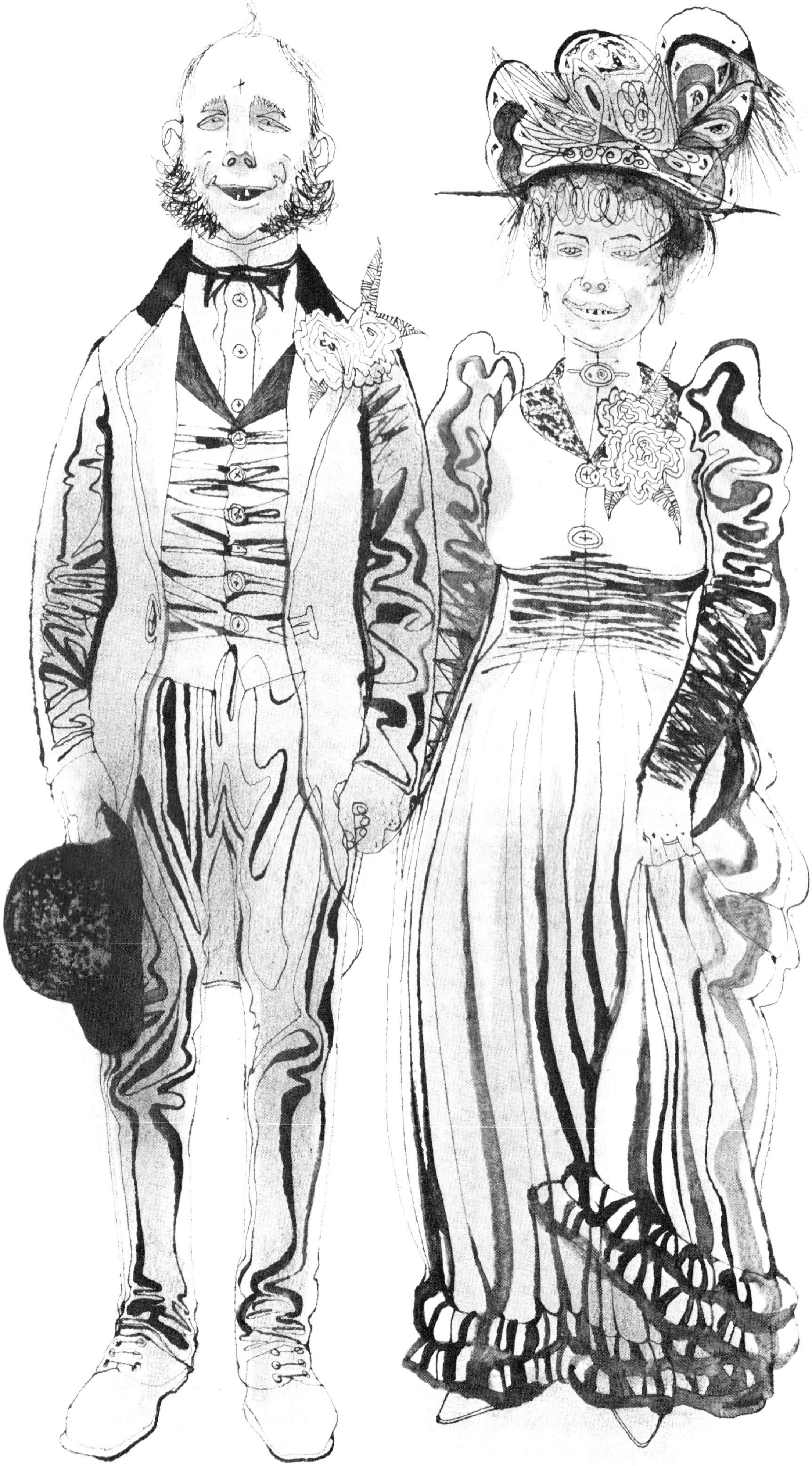

I'm Henery the Eighth, I Am!

1 You don't know who you're looking at; now have a look at me!
   I'm a bit of a nob, I am, belong to royaltee.
   I'll tell you how it came about: I married Widow Burch,
   And I was King of England, when I toddled out of church.
   Outside the people started shouting 'Hip-hoo-ray!'
   Said I, 'Get down upon your knees, it's Coronation day!'

   I'm Henery the Eighth I am!
   Henery the Eighth, I am, I am!
   I got married to the widow next door,
   She's been married seven times before.
   Ev'ry one was a Henery,
   She wouldn't have a Willie or a Sam.
   I'm her eighth old man named Henery,
   I'm Henery the Eighth, I am!

2 I left the 'Duke of Cumberland', a pub up in the town
   Soon with one or two moochers I was holding up the 'Crown'.
   I sat upon the bucket that the carmen think their own;
   Surrounded by my subjects I was sitting on the throne.
   Out came the potman saying, 'Go on, home to bed!'
   Said I, 'Now say another word, and off 'll go your head!'

3 Now at the Waxwork Exhibition not so long ago
   I was sitting among the kings I made a lovely show.
   To good old Queen Elizabeth I shouted, 'Wot-cher Liz!'
   While people poked my ribs and said, 'I wonder who this is!'
   One said, 'It's Charley Peace!' and then I got the spike.
   I shouted, 'Show yer ignorance!' as waxy as you like.

I'M HENERY THE EIGHTH, I AM!

Bright tempo
VERSE

Words and music by Murray and Weston

You don't know who you're look-ing at; now have a look at me!__ I'm a bit of a nob, I am, be-long to roy-al-tee.__ I'll tell you how it came a-bout: I mar-ried Wi-dow Burch,__ And I was King of Eng-land, when I tod-dled out of church.__ Out-side the peo-ple start-ed shout-ing 'Hip-hoo-ray!'__ Said I, 'Get down up-on your knees, it's Cor-on-a-tion day!'

CHORUS

I'm Hen-er-y the Eighth I am!__ Hen-er-y the Eighth, I am, I am!__

Copyright by FRANCIS, DAY & HUNTER LTD., London.

I got married to the wid-ow next door, She's been mar-ried sev-en times before. Ev-'ry one was a Hen-er-y, She would-n't have a Wil-lie or a Sam. I'm her eighth old man named Hen-er-y I'm Hen-er-y the Eighth, I am!' I am!'

Sing Me to Sleep

Collected by Charles Keeping

'Sing me to sleep' I heard a man bawl,
At a sub-ur-ban mus-ic hall. He was a
ten-or, so brave and so bold, He had a
voice like a crow with a cold. 'Sing me to
sleep' I heard a man cry, 'Sing me to sleep' with a
tear in his eye. Then came a half-brick, slung by a
sweep, Fell on his napp-er and put him to sleep.

This arrangement © 1975 by BRITISH AND CONTINENTAL MUSIC AGENCIES LTD.

SING ME TO SLEEP

1 'Sing me to sleep' I heard a man bawl,
  At a suburban music hall.
  He was a tenor, so brave and so bold,
  He had a voice like a crow with a cold.

2 'Sing me to sleep' I heard a man cry,
  'Sing me to sleep' with a tear in his eye.
  Then came a half-brick, slung by a sweep,
  Fell on his napper and put him to sleep.

Boiled Beef and Carrots

Words and music by Charles Collins and Fred Murray

Allegretto

VERSE

When I was a nipper only six months old, My mother and my father too, They did-n't know what to wean me on, They were both in a dreadful stew; They thought of tripe, they thought of steak, Or a little bit of old cod's roe, I said, 'Pop round to the old cook-shop, I know what 'll make me grow.'

CHORUS

Boiled beef and carrots, Boiled beef and carrots. That's the stuff for your 'Dar-by-kel', Makes you fat and it keeps you well, Don't live like veg-e-

Revised Edition Copyright 1939 by B. FELDMAN & CO., London, England.

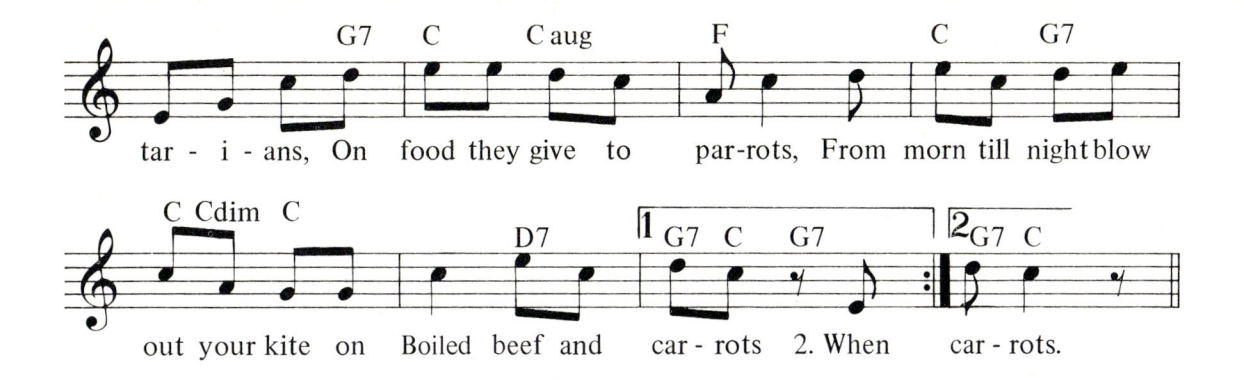

BOILED BEEF AND CARROTS

1. When I was a nipper only six months old,
My mother and my father too,
They didn't know what to wean me on,
They were both in a dreadful stew;
They thought of tripe, they thought of steak,
Or a little bit of old cod's roe,
I said, 'Pop round to the old cookshop,
I know what'll make me grow.'

   Boiled beef and carrots,
   Boiled beef and carrots.
   That's the stuff for your 'Darby-kel',
   Makes you fat and it keeps you well,
   Don't live like vegetarians,
   On food they give to parrots,
   From morn till night blow out your kite on
   Boiled beef and carrots.

2. When I got married to Eliza Brown,
A funny little girl next door,
We went to Brighton for the week,
Then we both toddled home once more;
My pals all met me in the pub,
Said a fellow to me, 'What cher, Fred,
What did you have for your honeymoon?'
So just for a lark I said:

3. We've got a lodger he's an artful cove,
'I'm very very queer,' he said.
We sent for the doctor, he came round,
And he told him to jump in bed.
The poor chap said, 'I do feel bad',
Then my mother with a tear replied,
'What would you like for a "Pick me up"?'
He jumped out of bed and cried:

4. I am the father of a lovely pair
Of kiddies, and they're nice fat boys;
They're twins, you can't tell which is which,
Like a pair of saveloys,
We had them christened in the week,
When the Parson put them on his knee,
I said, 'As they've got ginger hair,
Now I want their names to be:

A Comical Cock

Collected by Charles Keeping

One Sunday afternoon I thought I'd go for a walk, I had a bowl down Petticoat Lane To hear the people talk. I had but three and six, I walked into a shop, I gave it to a nice young man Who handed me a cock-a-doodle do. Well, it's nothing to do with you, It's a comical cock-you all know what, So run away, run away, do. Well, tra-la-la-la-la, run away, run away, do.

This arrangement © 1975 by BRITISH AND CONTINENTAL MUSIC AGENCIES LTD.

A COMICAL COCK

1. One Sunday afternoon
   I thought I'd go for a walk,
   I had a bowl down Petticoat Lane
   To hear the people talk.
   I had but three and six,
   I walked into a shop,
   I gave it to a nice young man
   Who handed me a cock–a-doodle-do.

   Well, it's nothing to do with you,
   It's a comical cock – you all know what,
   So run away, run away, do.
   Well, tra-la-la-la, run away, run away, do.

2. I put me cock under me arm,
   I hadn't far to go,
   I gave the bird a bit of a squeeze,
   The bugger began to crow.
   A lady passing by,
   It gave her a bit of a shock,
   She said 'Young man, if you don't watch out
   You're going to lose your cock–a-doodle-do.'

3. That very same afternoon
   I thought I'd go for a roam,
   I got into a rowing boat
   And went out on the foam.
   There came one hell of a wave,
   The boat began to rock,
   I fell into the water
   And a fish got hold of me cock–a-doodle-do.

4. Dear friends, I must be going,
   I can no longer stay,
   To sing you another verse
   Would take me half the day.
   But before I leave
   I'd like to show me stock.
   Is there any young lady in the room
   Would care to look at me cock–a-doodle-do?

The Moon Shines Tonight on Charlie Chaplin

Collected by Charles Keeping

For the moon shines to-night on Char-lie Chap-lin,
His boots are crack-ing, for the want of black-'ning
And his lit-tle bag-gy trous-ers they want mend-ing,
Be-fore they send him to the Dar-dan-elles. The
moon shines down on Char-lie Chap-lin, He's go-ing
bar-my to join the ar-my, And his
lit-tle kha-ki trous-ers they want mend-ing,
Be-fore they send him to the Dar-dan-elles.

Copyright by B. FELDMAN & CO., London, England.

THE MOON SHINES TONIGHT ON CHARLIE CHAPLIN

1 For the moon shines tonight on Charlie Chaplin,
His boots are cracking, for the want of black'ning
And his little baggy trousers they want mending,
Before they send him to the Dardanelles.

2 The moon shines down on Charlie Chaplin,
He's going barmy to join the army,
And his little khaki trousers they want mending,
Before they send him to the Dardanelles.

The Amateur Whitewasher

Moderato

Words and music by Murray and Leigh

I'm a ve-ry han-dy man, To save a bit of 'oof's my plan; One day last week I said to my wife, 'Our yard wants a wash up - on my life. So I'll go and do the job,' And I did so help me bob! Made a pail of white-wash, set to work, And the old girl helped me like a Turk:

CHORUS

Slap - dab! Slap - dab! up and down the brick - work, Slap - dab! all day long, In and out the cor - ners, Round the John - ny Horn - ers, We were a pair of fair clean gon - ers, Slab - dab! Slap! with the

Reproduced by permission of ASCHERBERG, HOPWOOD & CREW LTD.

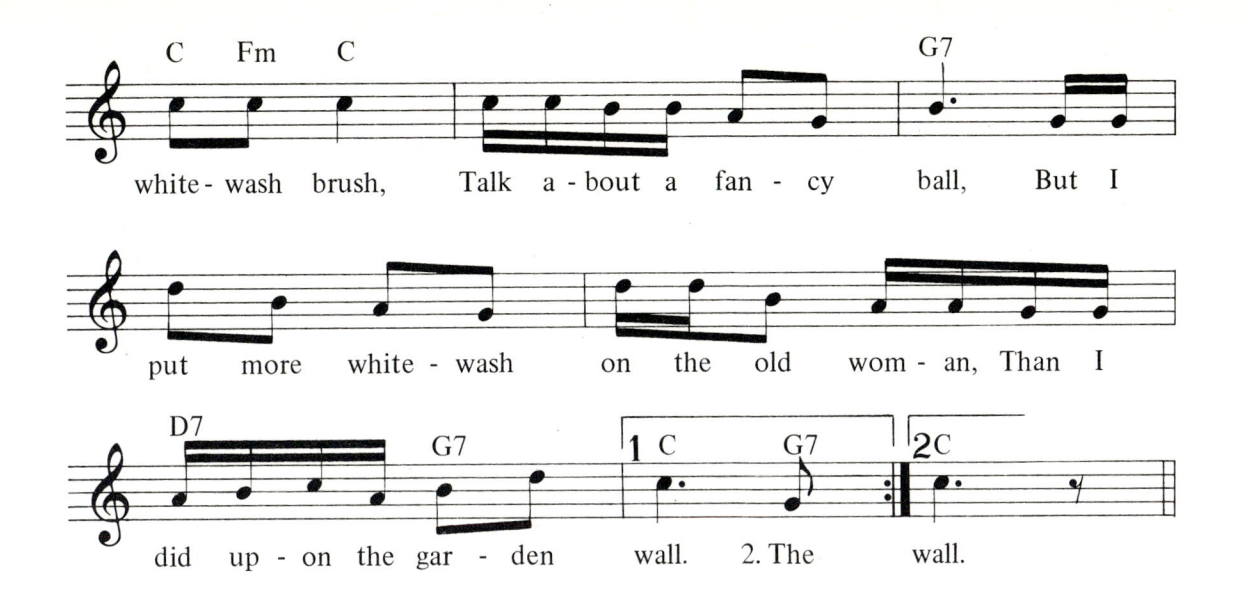

THE AMATEUR WHITEWASHER

1   I'm a very handy man,
    To save a bit of 'oof's my plan;
    One day last week I said to my wife,
    'Our yard wants a wash up on my life.
    So I'll go and do the job,'
    And I did so help me bob!
    Made a pail of whitewash, set to work,
    And the old girl helped me like a Turk.

   Slap–dab! Slap–dab! up and down the brick-work,
   Slap–dab! all day long,
   In and out the corners,
   Round the Johnny Horners,
   We were a pair of fair clean goners,
   Slap–dab! Slap! with the whitewash brush,
   Talk about a fancy ball,
   But I put more whitewash on the old woman,
   Than I did upon the garden wall.

2   The missis, I must now confess,
    She put me in her old night dress,
    Her night cap, too, she made me wear,
    She was dress'd like me, so we look'd a pair.
    She held up the pail so high,
    And I made that whitewash fly,
    Ev'ry now and then I heard a squall,
    I was taking the old girl's face for the wall:

3 Feeling very dry just here,
 We went to get a drop of beer;
 And the kids from the house next door, I think,
 Attracted by the whitewash, came and had a drink;
 There's got to be an inquest now,
 And I am in a dreadful row,
 I have done with economical schemes,
 For ev'ry night in all my dreams:

I'm a Navvy

Collected by Charles Keeping

I'm a nav-vy, I'm a nav-vy, work-ing on the line, I get five and twen-ty bob a week, and all my ov-er-time. Pease pud-ding and gra-vy, ev-'ry din-ner time, That's what a nav-vy gets for work-ing on the line.

This arrangement © 1975 by BRITISH AND CONTINENTAL MUSIC AGENCIES LTD.

I'M A NAVVY

1. I'm a navvy, I'm a navvy, working on the line,
   I get five and twenty bob a week, and all my overtime.
   Pease pudding and gravy, ev'ry dinner time,
   That's what a navvy gets for working on the line.

2. I'm a navvy, I'm a navvy, working on the line,
   Chopping up the worms, and making one worm into nine,
   Some jobs are rotten jobs, and some jobs are fine,
   When you're a navvy, you're a navvy working on the line.

Feeding the Ducks on the Pond

Collected by Charles Keeping

Feed - ing the ducks on the pond (Quack! Quack!)

Feed - ing the ducks on the pond (Quack! Quack!) Now

it's a great art feed - ing ducks I de - clare,

Watch - ing one duck don't get more than its share. It's

far more ex - cit - ing to me Than when I was

out there at Mons. When the ducks are all

fed, I will send for more bread, Then I'll

come back and feed all the swans.

Copyright 1919 by B. FELDMAN & CO., London, England.

FEEDING THE DUCKS ON THE POND

Feeding the ducks on the pond (Quack! Quack!)
Feeding the ducks on the pond (Quack! Quack!)

1 Now it's a great art feeding ducks I declare,
Watching one duck don't get more than its share.
It's far more exciting to me
Than when I was out there at Mons.
When the ducks are all fed,
I will send for more bread,
Then I'll come back and feed all the swans.

(Spoken with vamped piano accompaniment)
'Arf a minute, just a minute, now this one is true,
The other morning for a ramble I went to the zoo.
Saw the lions, in the monkey house than I did roam,
Blowed if they didn't shout 'Father's come home.'

(Whisper)
2 Keep it as quiet as you can – not a word – mustn't shout,
I had to kiss all the young apes and I'm frightened
It might get about.
Just a minute, just a minute,
Half a crown all I charge to make a coal barge
Look a steamer – say, how's that?
Where the funnel should be, I just stick my high hat.

When I Went for a Soldier

Collected by Charles Keeping

When I went for a sol-dier, Moth-er she got drunk, fa-ther did a bunk, And the 'Old Dun Cow' caught fire. Down came the lod-ger with a broom, But he did not stop there long, When he saw my sword, 'Oh dear! Oh lord! A-no-ther sil-ly sod gone wrong.' no-ther sil-ly sod gone wrong.'

This arrangement © 1975 by BRITISH AND CONTINENTAL MUSIC AGENCIES LTD.

WHEN I WENT FOR A SOLDIER

When I went for a soldier,
Mother she got drunk, father did a bunk,
And the 'Old Dun Cow' caught fire.
Down came the lodger with a broom,
But he did not stop there long,
When he saw my sword, 'Oh dear! Oh lord!
Another silly sod gone wrong.'

SENTIMENTAL SONGS

Liza, You Are a Lady

Collected by Charles Keeping

This arrangement © 1975 by BRITISH AND CONTINENTAL MUSIC AGENCIES LTD.

LIZA, YOU ARE A LADY

Liza, you are a lady,
You fancy yourself you do.
Way down a lane so shady,
You will marry the Lord knows who.
Don't try to put the swank on,
For you know it's only sham.
Think of where you used to be,
Down at Pinkses factory,
All amongst the marmalade and jam.

Liza, It's a Beautiful Starry Night

Liza, it's a beautiful starry night,
Liza, the moon is shining bright.
I've called round to see if you'll elope;
Slip on something, if it's only a bar o' soap.
Liza, never mind abaht yer clothes,
I ain't a bit particular,
Fine fevvers make fine birds,
But I'd sooner 'ave yer, Liza, as you are.

LIZA, IT'S A BEAUTIFUL STARRY NIGHT

Collected by Charles Keeping

Li - za, it's a beau - ti - ful star - 'ry night,

Li - za, the moon is shin - ing bright,

I've called round to see if you'll e - lope; Slip on

some - thing, if it's on - ly a bar o' soap.

Li - za, nev - er mind a - baht yer clothes,

I ain't a bit par - tic - u - lar,

Fine fev - vers make fine birds, But I'd

soon - er 'ave yer, Li - za, as you are.

88

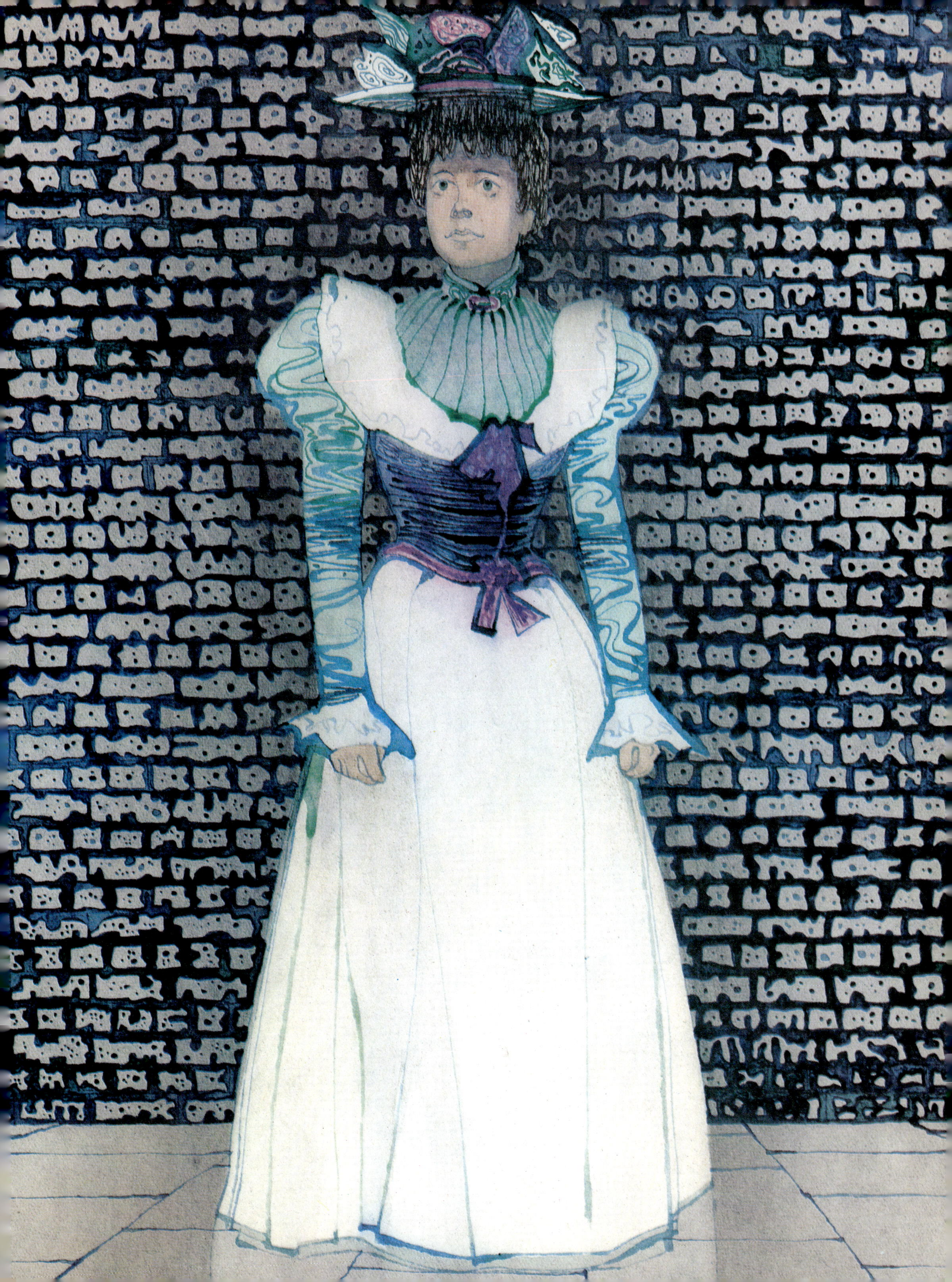

Liza Johnston

Collected by Charles Keeping

Copyright 1901 by FRANCIS, DAY & HUNTER LTD., London.

LIZA JOHNSTON

Liza, you are my donna,
You are my little peach,
Meet me outside the fish shop
And I will buy yer a penn'orth of each;
Gawd love yer,
No bloke shall come and kiss yer
Or for him I would go,
And if I should lose my temper
Then it's 'What-'o, Liza Johnston – say, what-'o!'

If Those Lips Could Only Speak

Valse moderato
VERSE F
Words and music by Charles Ridgewell and Will Godwin

He stood in a beau-ti-ful man-sion, Sur-

Gm   C7

round-ed by rich-es un-told;___ He gazed at a

beau-ti-ful pic-ture___ That hung in a frame of

F   Dm   B♭   A7

gold.___ 'Twas a pic-ture of a la-dy___ So

B♭   Dm   G

beau-ti-ful, young and fair.___ To the beau-ti-ful

C   Cdim C   G7   C7

life-like fea-tures He murmured in sad des-pair.___

CHORUS F

'If those lips could on-ly speak,___ If those eyes could

Ddim Gm   C7

on-ly see;___ If those beau-ti-ful gold-en tress-es___

This arrangement © 1975 by BRITISH AND CONTINENTAL MUSIC AGENCIES LTD.

IF THOSE LIPS COULD ONLY SPEAK

1 He stood in a beautiful mansion,
Surrounded by riches untold;
He gazed at a beautiful picture
That hung in a frame of gold.
'Twas a picture of a lady
So beautiful, young and fair.
To the beautiful lifelike features
He murmured in sad despair.

> 'If those lips could only speak,
> If those eyes could only see;
> If those beautiful golden tresses
> Were there in reality;
> Could I only take your hand,
> As I did when you took my name!
> But it's only a beautiful picture
> In a beautiful golden frame.'

2 With all his great pow'r and his riches,
   He knows he can never replace
   One thing in the mansion that's absent,
   His wife's tender smiling face.
   And each time he sees her picture
   These same words you'll hear him say:
   'All my wealth I would freely forfeit
   And toil for you night and day.'

3 He sat there and gazed at the painting,
   Then slumbered forgetting all pain;
   And there in that mansion, in fancy,
   She stood by his side again.
   Then his lips they softly murmured
   The name of his once sweet bride;
   With his eyes fixed upon the picture
   He awoke from his dream and cried.

That's Where My Love Lies Dreaming

That's where my love lies dreaming,
Dreaming the hours away.
Absolutely speechless up in London Town,
Lying in the gutter without a frown,
Whosoever said that he could fight,
The backers all were screaming,
He only fought a round or two and he felt queer,
All his teeth were missing and 'arf an ear,
Lying in the gutter, blind to the world,
That's where my love lies dreaming.

THAT'S WHERE MY LOVE LIES DREAMING

Collected by Charles Keeping

That's where my love lies dream-ing, Dream-ing the ho-urs a-way. Ab-sol-ute-ly speech-less up in Lon-don Town, Ly-ing in the gut-ter with-out a frown, Who-so-ev-er said that he could fight, The back-ers all were scream-ing, He on-ly fought a round or two and he felt queer, All his teeth were miss-ing and 'arf an ear, Ly-ing in the gut-ter, blind to the world, That's where my love lies dream-ing.

This arrangement © 1975 by BRITISH AND CONTINENTAL MUSIC AGENCIES LTD.

BOXING
ARENA
BOXING
ARENA
SUNDAY
BOXING 3pm
MONDAY . THURSDAY
BOXING & WRESTLING 8
GYMNASIUM
OPEN TO THE PUBLIC
SATURDAY
BOXING & WRESTLING 8PM
F. H. AYRES LTD
18 ALDERSGATE STREET LONDON EC1
MANUFACTURES OF SPORTS & GAMES
PHONE
WRESTLINGS
OF CHAMPIONSHIP CLASS
BOOKED SEATS
ARE BEST SEATS
WRESTLING
TUESDAY
Charlie Clarke

The Sunshine of Your Smile

Moderato
VERSE

Words by Leonard Cooke. Music by Lilian Ray

Dear face that holds so sweet a smile for me,
Were you not mine, how dark the world would be!
I know no light a-bove, that could re-place
Love's ra-diant sun-shine in your dear, dear face.

CHORUS

Give me your smile, the love-light in your eyes,
Life could not hold a fair-er Pa-ra-dise!
Give me the right to love you all the while,
My world for-ev-er, the sun-shine of your smile!

Copyright 1913 by FRANCIS, DAY & HUNTER LTD., London.

THE SUNSHINE OF YOUR SMILE

1 Dear face that holds so sweet a smile for me,
   Were you not mine, how dark the world would be!
   I know no light above, that could replace
   Love's radiant sunshine in your dear, dear face.

   Give me your smile, the lovelight in your eyes,
   Life could not hold a fairer Paradise!
   Give me the right to love you all the while,
   My world forever, the sunshine of your smile!

2 Shadows may fall upon the land and sea,
   Sunshine from all the world may hidden be.
   But I shall see no cloud across the sun,
   Your smile shall light my life, till life is done.

Sons of the Sea

Words and music by Felix McGlennon

Tempo di Marcia

Sons of the sea! All British born!
Sailing ev'ry ocean, Laughing foes to scorn.
They may build their ships, my lads, and think they know the game,
But they can't build boys of the bulldog breed, Who made old England's name.

Copyright 1897 by Chas. Sheard & Co.
HERMAN DAREWSKI MUSIC PUBLISHING CO. LTD., London, England.

SONS OF THE SEA

1 Have you heard the talk of foreign pow'rs
Building ships increasingly?
Do you know they watch this Isle of ours?
Watch their chance unceasingly?
Have you heard the millions they will spend
Strengthening their fleets, and why?
They imagine they can break or bend
The nation that has often made them fly.
But one thing we possess, they forget, they forget;
The lads in blue they've met,
Often met, often met.

Sons of the sea!
All British born!
Sailing ev'ry ocean,
Laughing foes to scorn.
They may build their ships, my lads, and
  think they know the game,
But they can't build boys of the bulldog breed,
Who made old England's name.

2 Do you know they threaten to combine,
   Three to one's their bravery?
   Do you know they'd like to sweep the brine,
   Bind us lads in slavery?
   Have you heard they think that plates of steel,
   Plates of steel and guns will do?
   But we know 'twas British hearts of oak
   In ev'ry battle pull'd us safely through:
   For one thing we possess, they forget, they forget;
   The lads in blue they've met,
   Often met, often met.

3 If they'd know why Britons rule the waves,
   If they'd solve the mystery,
   If they'd know the deeds of Britain's braves,
   Let them read their history.
   Let them search the bottom of the seas
   Where their battered hulks now lie,
   Let them build their puny ships of war,
   We build men prepared to do or die.
   There's one thing we possess, they forget, they forget;
   The lads in blue they've met,
   Often met, often met.

Granny

Slowly – Rubato
VERSE

Collected by Charles Keeping

I know an old fash-ioned la - dy, Time's made her old and grey, And just like an - y old la - dy, She thinks she's in the way. Some - times she sighs, Some - times she cries, Some - times she smiles, when I say:

CHORUS

'Gran - ny, you're my mam - my's mam - my, I owe a lot to you. Gran - ny, you gave me my mam - my, The great - est thing a

This arrangement © 1975 by BRITISH AND CONTINENTAL MUSIC AGENCIES LTD.

GRANNY

1. I know an old-fashioned lady,
   Time's made her old and grey,
   And just like any old lady,
   She thinks she's in the way.
   Sometimes she sighs,
   Sometimes she cries,
   Sometimes she smiles, when I say:

   'Granny, you're my mammy's mammy,
   I owe a lot to you.
   Granny, you gave me my mammy,
   The greatest thing a granny could do.
   I'd rather own the silver in your tresses
   Than all the gold this great big world possesses.
   Granny, you're my mammy's mammy,
   I'm mighty proud of you.'

When the Summer Comes Again

Slowly
Words and music by Harry Bedford

Oh! won't we have some mon-ey, Nell, When the sum-mer comes a-gain, Life will be all hon-ey, gell, When the sum-mer comes a-gain; We shall roam all round the coun-try, With pret-ty flow'rs, sun-shine or rain, Straight! we'll buy up Cov-ent Gar-den, When the

CHORUS

sum-mer comes a-gain. When the sum-mer comes a-gain ___ And the pret-ty flow'rs are grow-ing, ___ The ___ sun-shine af-ter rain, ___ The sum-mer breez-es blow-ing; ___

Copyright by FRANCIS, DAY & HUNTER LTD., London.

WHEN THE SUMMER COMES AGAIN

1. Oh! won't we have some money, Nell,
   When the summer comes again,
   Life will be all honey, gell,
   When the summer comes again;
   We shall roam all round the country,
   With pretty flow'rs, sunshine or rain,
   Straight! we'll buy up Covent Garden,
   When the summer comes again.

   When the summer comes again
   And the pretty flow'rs are growing,
   The sunshine after rain,
   The summer breezes blowing;
   Then to roam around the country
   With a girl who's ever willing
   I can buy and she can cry,
   'Three pots a shilling!'

2. 'Sweet window flow'rs' then you'll cry, Nell,
   When the summer comes again,
   Toffs from us will buy 'em, gell,
   When the summer comes again;
   For I knows the best of houses,
   Where lots of profit we can gain,
   Splendid clothes they'll give for flowers,
   When the summer comes again.

3. Oh! won't we turn out dashing, Nell,
   When the summer comes again,
   Folks will talk about it, gell,
   When the summer comes again;
   You shall dress in 'broshey' velvet,
   Me a silver watch and chain,
   Let coves see we knows our book Nell,
   When the summer comes again.

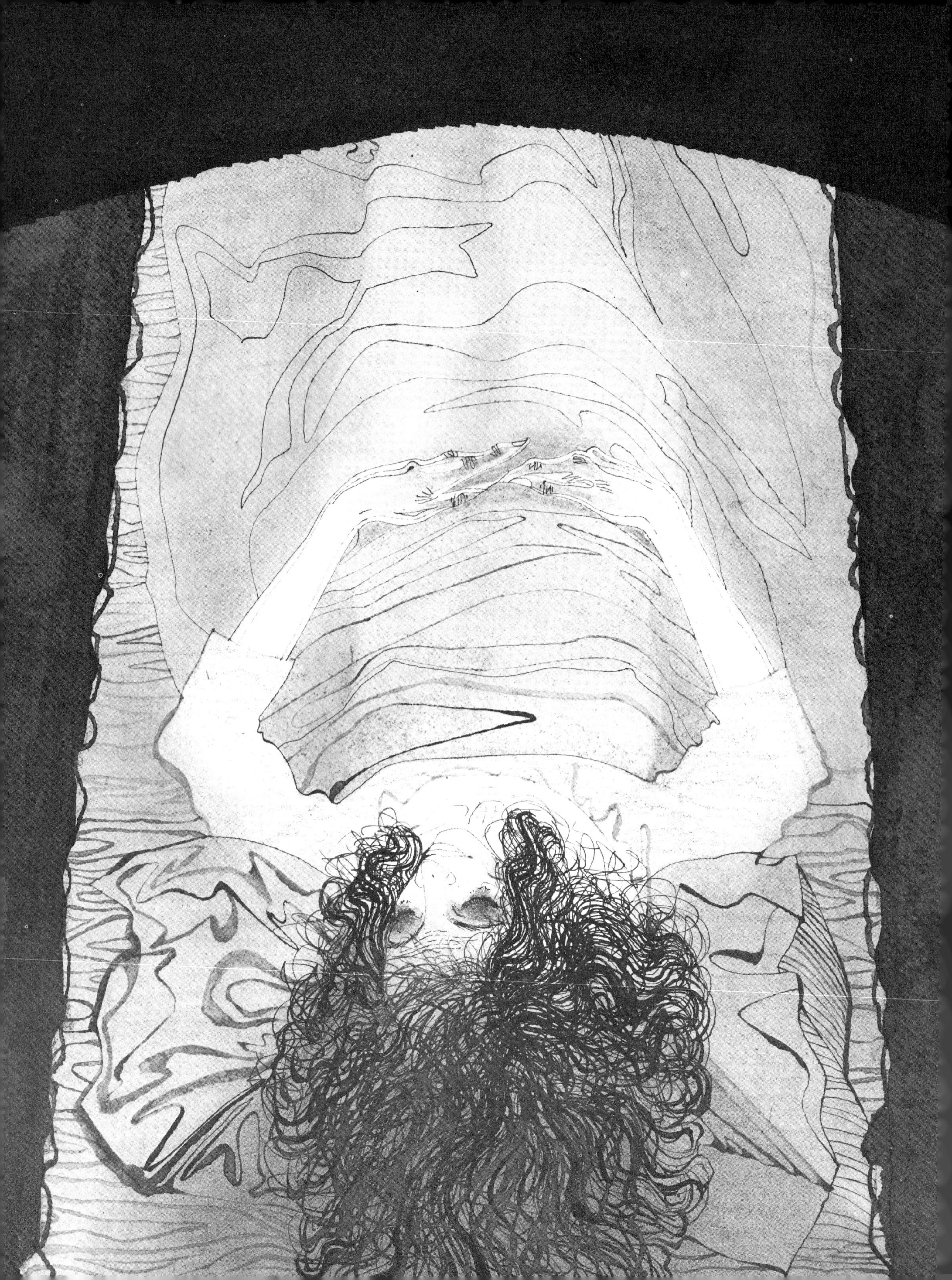

Whilst the Dance Goes On

Collected by Charles Keeping

VERSE

A-midst a scene of great splen-dour___ There in a ball-room so bright___ Mer-ry and gay were the danc-ers___ No thought of sorr-ow to-night.___ Keep-ing in time with the mus-ic___ Dan-cing from eve-ning till dawn___ Hap-py are they, joy-ous and gay, Whilst the dance goes on.___

CHORUS

Whilst the mus-ic is play-ing___ In the grand ball-room,___ Whilst each heart beats soft-ly___

HERMAN DAREWSKI MUSIC PUBLISHING CO. LTD., London, England.

WHILST THE DANCE GOES ON

1. Amidst a scene of great splendour
   There in a ballroom so bright
   Merry and gay were the dancers
   No thought of sorrow tonight.
   Keeping in time with the music
   Dancing from evening till dawn
   Happy are they, joyous and gay,
   Whilst the dance goes on.

   Whilst the music is playing
   In the grand ballroom,
   Whilst each heart beats softly
   To the old sweet tune,
   Whilst the hours are passing,
   Fleeting one by one,
   They have no thought of tomorrow
   Whilst the dance goes on.

2. But there was one of these dancers
   One with a beautiful face
   Laughing and chaffing so gaily,
   Dancing with such careless grace.
   She had no firm hand to guide her,
   No one to shield her from harm
   She is alone – husband at home –
   Whilst the dance goes on.

3. 'You shall not go to the ball love
   Stay with our baby tonight,'
   Rang in the ears of this lady
   Whose eyes they shone clear and bright.
   What cares she for home or for baby
   As long as she's queen of the ball?
   She is alone – baby at home –
   Whilst the dance goes on.

4. Too soon the ball it was over
   Home she approached at last
   There at the door stands her husband
   Whose tears they fell thick and fast,
   But not a word has he spoken,
   Gently he leads his wife in,
   There on the bed – her baby lay dead
   Whilst the dance goes on.

Jeerusalem's Dead!

Words by Brian Daly. Music by John Crook

Mournfully
VERSE

I've 'ad four 'arf-pints at the 'Mag-pie an' Stump', An' two goes o' rum jes ter keep up my sper-rits; My mince-pies are wa-ter-in' jes like a pump, An' they're red as a fer-rit's. Cos why? 'Tain't the mis-sus nor kids wot I've lost, But one wot I care-ful-*lie* doc-tored and fed; The nuss-in' an' watch-in' 'as turned out a frost, The Jee-ru-sa-lem's dead! Yer

CHORUS

won't see 'im pul-lin' the bar-rer no more, Wi'

Copyright by REYNOLDS MUSIC, London. All Rights Reserved.

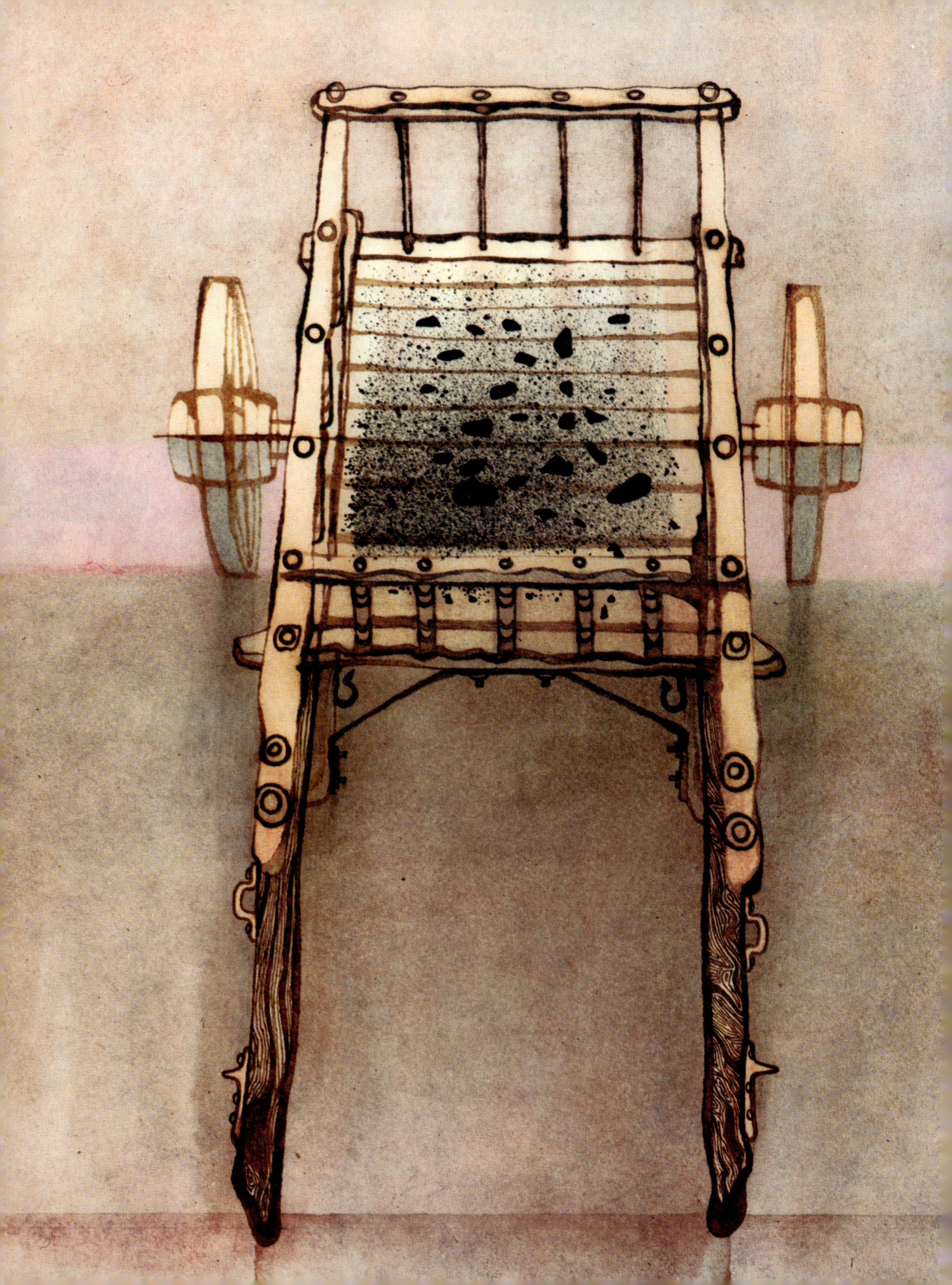

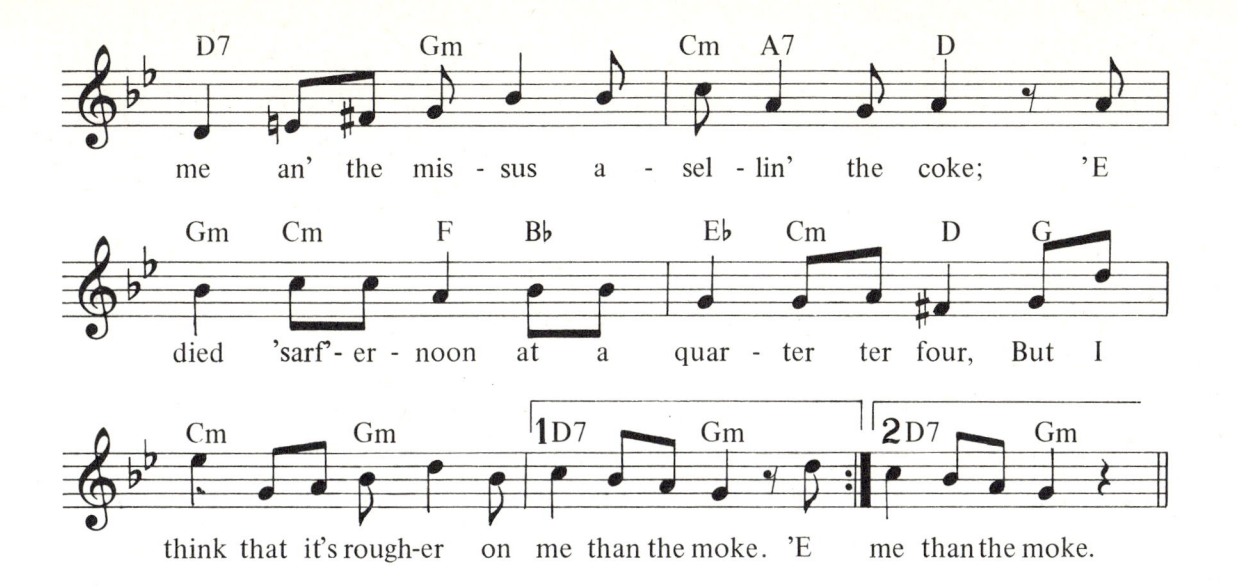

me an' the mis-sus a-sel-lin' the coke; 'E died 'sarf'-er-noon at a quar-ter ter four, But I think that it's rough-er on me than the moke. 'E me than the moke.

JEERUSALEM'S DEAD!

1. I've 'ad four 'arf-pints at the 'Magpie-an'-Stump',
   An' two goes o' rum jes ter keep up my sperrits;
   My mince-pies are waterin' jes like a pump,
   An' they're red as a ferrit's.
   Cos why? – 'Tain't the missus nor kids wot I've lost,
   But one wot I carefullie doctored and fed;
   The nussin' an' watchin' 'as turned out a frost,
   The Jeerusalem's dead!

   Yer won't see 'im pullin' the barrer no more,
   Wi' me an' the missus a-sellin' the coke;
   'E died 's arf'ernoon at a quarter ter four,
   But I think that it's rougher on me than the moke.

2. 'E 'ad a big 'eart and a strong pair o' 'eels,
   A temper as short as was e'er manifactured;
   In 'arness 'e used ter do 'ornpipes an' reels,
   An' my ribs 'e once fractured!
   'E bit like the devil, and eat like a 'orse,
   An' orfen 'e'd try ter stand up on 'is 'ead;
   It's all over now wiv 'is tricks an' 'is sauce,
   The Jeerusalem's dead!

3   I stroked 'is old 'ead as 'e laid in the stall,
    An' somehow or other I felt I must kiss 'im!
    I've a wife an' some youngsters! 'E wasn't quite all,
    But I know I shall miss 'im.
    There's one thing I'm certain, 'is grub was the best,
    An' I've gone short myself ter purvide 'im a bed;
    Come an' 'ave 'arf a pint – there's a lump in my chest,
    The Jeerusalem's dead!

Silver Bells

1   In the hush of eventide,
    Sitting by my cottage door,
    Fancy softly seems to glide
    Backwards to the days of yore.
    Once again I see the dell,
    Wander through the flowery lea,
    To the sound of silver bells,
    Silver bells of memory.

    Silver bells, silver bells,
    Silver bells of memory,
    Silver bells, silver bells,
    Silver bells of memory.

2   Many faces have grown old,
    Many forms been laid to rest
    Underneath the churchyard mould,
    Those we love the most and best.
    Then again I hear the swell,
    Floating o'er the winds to me,
    'Tis the sound of silver bells,
    Silver bells of memory.

SILVER BELLS

Collected by Charles Keeping

VERSE

In the hush of ev - en - tide, Sit - ting by my cott - age door, Fan - cy soft - ly seems to glide Back - wards to the days of yore. Once a - gain I see the dell, Wan - der through the flow - ery lea, To the sound of sil - ver bells, Sil - ver bells of

CHORUS

mem - or - y. Sil - ver bells, sil - ver bells, Sil - ver bells of mem - or - y, _____ Sil - ver bells, sil - ver bells, Sil - ver bells of mem - or - y. _____

This arrangement © 1975 by BRITISH AND CONTINENTAL MUSIC AGENCIES LTD.

The Coster's Linnet

Allegretto con espress.

Words and music by Charles Seel

VERSE

You've all heard of Li-za's wed-ding, How she mar-ried my pal Bill, I was at the church and heard her Speak those mag-ic words 'I will'; When I saw her get-ting mar-ried, I thought I should go in-sane, When she chucked me up for him, My heart was broke with grief and pain. Once I had a moke and bar-row, And con-nec-tion next to none, But I took to drink and sold them, Ev-'ry-thing but this has gone.

Reproduced by permission of ASCHERBERG, HOPWOOD & CREW LTD.

CHORUS

It's only a simple linnet, Tho' for years it has been my 'pard', Tho' now we must part, it's breaking my heart, To sell him it seems very hard! He's woke me first thing in the morning, When out on my rounds I'd to start, It's a saying that's true, tho' it's not very new, 'The best of old friends must part.'

THE COSTER'S LINNET

1   You've all heard of Liza's wedding,
      How she married my pal Bill,
    I was at the church and heard her
      Speak those magic words – 'I will';
    When I saw her getting married,
      I thought I should go insane,
    When she chucked me up for him,
      My heart was broke with grief and pain.
    Once I had a moke and barrow,
      And connection next to none,
    But I took to drink and sold them,
      Ev'rything but this has gone.

   It's only a simple linnet,
      Tho' for years it has been my 'pard',
   Tho' now we must part, it's breaking my heart,
      To sell him it seems very hard!
   He's woke me first thing in the morning,
      When out on my rounds I'd to start,
   It's a saying that's true, tho' it's not very new,
      'The best of old friends must part.'

2   All went well till three months arter,
      Bill came home and found a note,
    'I have left you for another',
      Were the cruel words she wrote.
    Well, I've known her from a baby,
      Long before she learned to talk,
    When she was a doll in 'pinnies',
      I would teach her how to walk,
    Oft she'd come and feed my linnet,
      Make my little home look smart,
    Now, alas! there's nothing in it,
      With my old pal I must part.

3   Late last night we saw poor Liza,
      Gazing through the window pane,
    'Bill,' she cried, 'forgive me, take me,
      To your heart and home again.'
    'Bill,' I pleaded, 'overlook it
      Take her back, lad, if you can.'
    'No,' he cried, 'I'd sooner die first,
      Though a coster, I'm a man,'
    Then my linnet started singing,
      Like a voice from up above,
    Through that they're once more together,
      Happy in each other's love.

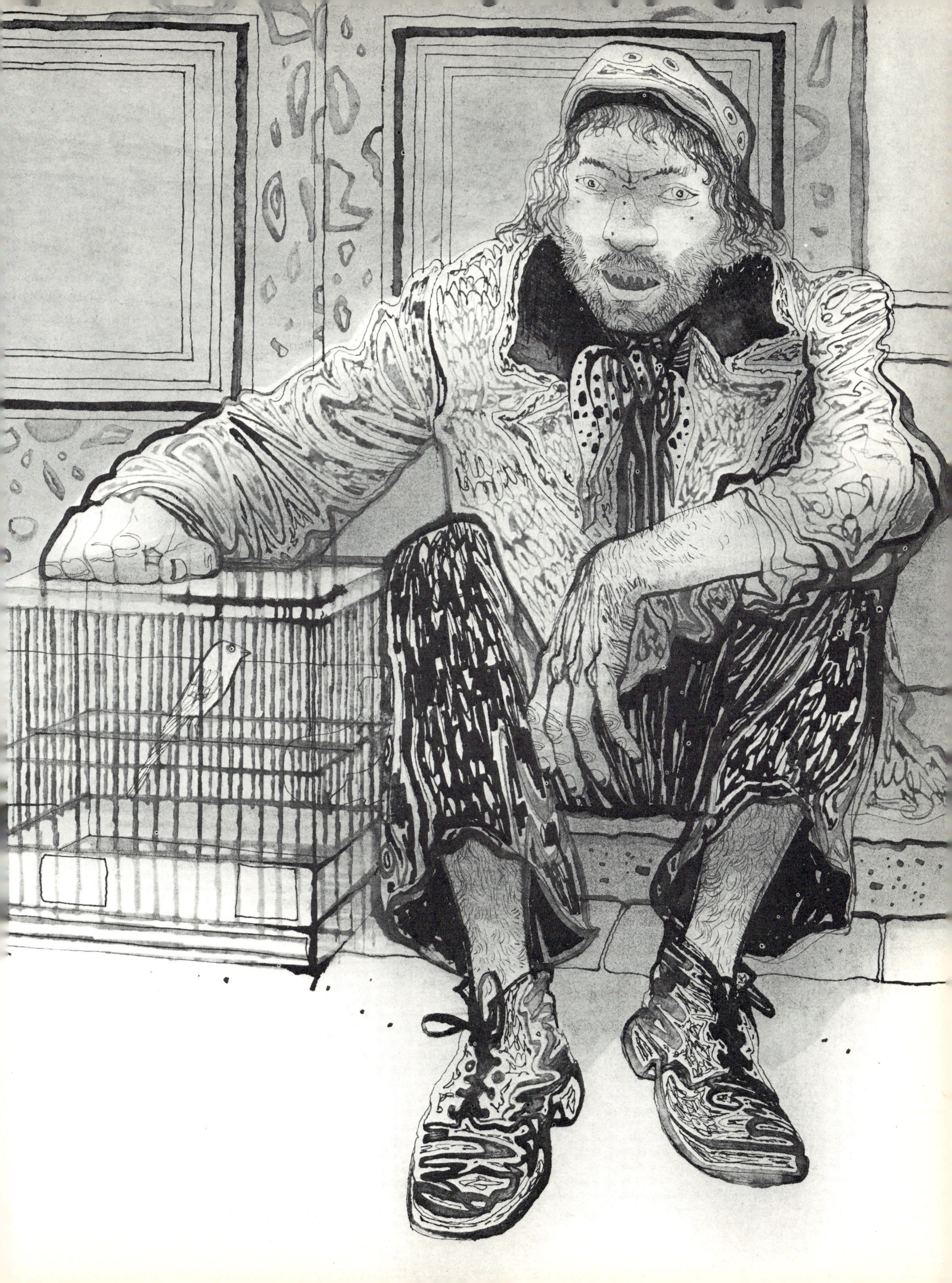

My Old Dutch

Moderato
VERSE

Words by Albert Chevalier. Music by Charles Ingle

I've got a pal, A reg'-lar out an' out-er, She's a dear good old gal, I'll tell yer all a-bout 'er; It's ma-ny years since fust we met, 'Er 'air was then as black as jet, It's whit-er now, but she don't fret, Not my old gal ___ We've

CHORUS

been to-geth-er now for for-ty years, An' it don't seem a day too much, ___ There ain't a la-dy liv-in' in the land, As I'd swop for my dear old Dutch. There ain't a la-dy liv-in' in the land, As I'd

Copyright 1893 by REYNOLDS MUSIC, London. All Rights Reserved.

swop for my dear old Dutch. Dutch.

MY OLD DUTCH

1 I've got a pal,
A reg'lar out an' outer,
She's a dear good old gal,
I'll tell you all about 'er;
It's many years since fust we met,
'Er 'air was then as black as jet,
It's whiter now, – but she don't fret,
Not my old gal . . .

We've been together now for forty years,
An' it don't seem a day too much,
There ain't a lady livin' in the land,
As I'd swop for my dear old Dutch.
There ain't a lady livin' in the land,
As I'd swop for my dear old Dutch.

2 I calls 'er Sal,
'Er proper name is Sairer,
An' yer may find a gal
As you'd consider fairer.
She ain't a' angel – she can start
A-jawin' till it makes yer smart,
She's just a *woman*, bless 'er 'eart,
Is my old gal!

3 Sweet fine old gal,
For worlds I wouldn't lose 'er,
She's a dear good old gal,
An' that's what made me choose 'er.
She's stuck to me through thick and thin,
When luck was out, when luck was in,
Ah! wot a wife to me she's been,
'An' wot a *pal!*

4 I sees yer Sal –
Yer pretty ribbons sportin'!
Many years now, old gal,
Since them young days of courtin'
I ain't a coward, still I trust
When we've to part, as part we must,
That Death may come and take me fust
To wait . . . my pal!

I Speak the Truth

Allegretto
VERSE

Collected by Charles Keeping

I'm full of joy, I'm full of joy, I feel just like a great big boy, I'm in love with my old dutch And she's in love with me. It's plain to see, it's plain to see, There must be some-thing wrong with me, Now that I am married and the proud fa-ther of three. My miss-us she is sweet and she is kind, I've al-ways got my dar-ling on my mind. I'm

CHORUS

al - ways think-ing of her, And she's al - ways

This arrangement © 1975 by BRITISH AND CONTINENTAL MUSIC AGENCIES LTD.

think-ing of me.   I al-ways know when she's think-ing of me Be-cause I know she's think-ing of me. I love her, I love her, yes I do, I love her when I've had one or two, But when I've had three or four I love her all the more. Ire-land is the place for Ir-ish stew. Now I

I SPEAK THE TRUTH

1 I'm full of joy, I'm full of joy,
I feel just like a great big boy,
I'm in love with my old dutch
And she's in love with me.
It's plain to see, it's plain to see,
There must be something wrong with me,
Now that I am married and the proud father of three.
My missus she is sweet and she is kind,
I've always got my darling on my mind.

> *I'm always thinking of her,*
> *And she's always thinking of me.*
> *I always know when she's thinking of me*
> *Because I know she's thinking of me.*
> *I love her, I love her, yes I do,*
> *I love her when I've had one or two,*
> *But when I've had three or four*
> *I love her all the more.*
> *Ireland is the place for Irish stew.*

2 I speak the truth, I speak the truth,
When I speak of my darling Ruth.
Her face it always haunts me
By night as well as day.
Oh, what a face, oh, what a face,
It helps to decorate the place.
It often comes in handy to frighten mice away.
If her face was her fortune you can bet
Nothing more than fourpence she would get.

> *I'm always thinking of her,*
> *And she's always thinking of me.*
> *I always know when she's thinking of me*
> *Because I know she's thinking of me.*
> *I love her, I love her, yes I do,*
> *I love her when I've had one or two,*
> *And when I come home on Sunday,*
> *What a time we have till Monday,*
> *And if you saw my old woman, so would you.*

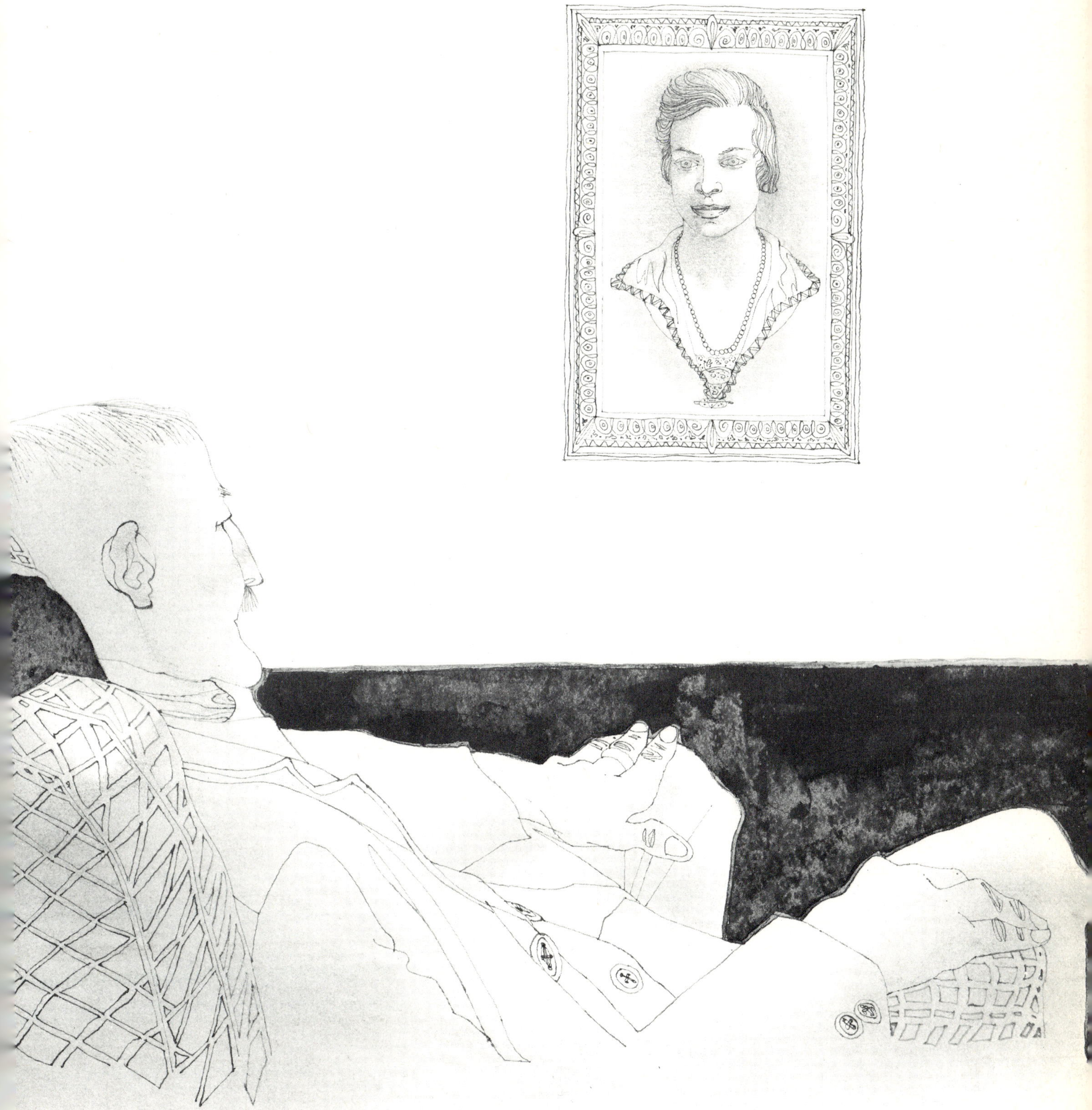

The Song of the Thrush

Words by Walter Hastings. Music by George le Brunn

Moderato

There fell a deep hush, as the song of the thrush Was heard by that mot-ley throng; And many a rough fell-ow's eyes were moist As the notes rang out clear and strong. Eyes light-ed up with a bright yearn-ing look, As the bird trill'd its beau-ti-ful lay; It brought to their minds dear old Eng-land and home, Thous-ands of miles a-way. There way.

Copyright 1897 by FRANCIS, DAY & HUNTER LTD., London.

THE SONG OF THE THRUSH

1 Years ago out in the wilds of Australia,
Out in the gold fields there once stood a camp;
The miners were made up of all sorts of classes,
With many a scape-grace and many a scamp;
Into their midst came a young man from England,
And with him he brought a small thrush in a cage;
To hear the bird sing they would crowd round in dozens,
The sweet little songster became quite a rage.

> *There fell a deep hush, as the song of the thrush*
> *Was heard by the motley throng;*
> *And many a rough fellow's eyes were moist*
> *As the notes rang out clear and strong.*
> *Eyes lighted up with a bright yearning look,*
> *As the bird trill'd its beautiful lay;*
> *It brought to their minds dear old England and home,*
> *Thousands of miles away.*

2 Rough were those miners, all fierce-looking fellows,
Yet they were human, and worshipp'd that bird.
When quarrels arose they would leave off and listen
If only the voice of their fav'rite they heard.
All round for miles he at last got quite famous,
On Sunday the miners would come from afar,
And many declar'd they prefer'd the bird's singing
To cards and the dice at the rough liquor bar.

3 Often they thought of the cornfields and meadows,
Many a shady and quiet little lane;
And hearts ach'd and yearn'd as they thought of some village,
And some they had dearly lov'd, but all in vain.
When the bird sang all those hard fellows listen'd,
Perhaps they got tired of the bird? no such thing!
As one rough express'd it, 'He came like an angel,
And makes you feel "good like" to hear that bird sing.'

A Sailor's Song

Collected by Charles Keeping

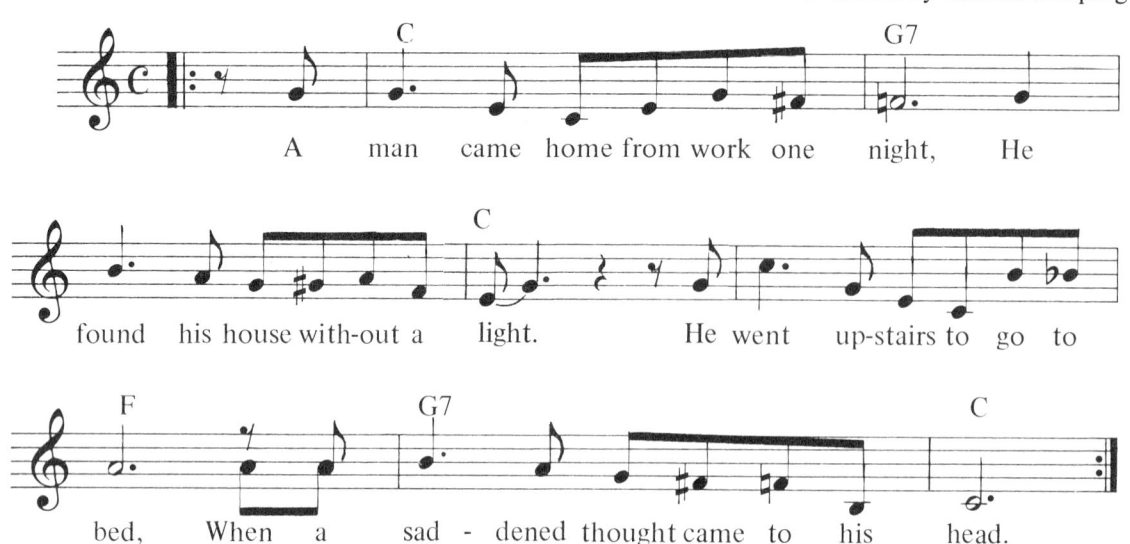

This arrangement © 1975 by BRITISH AND CONTINENTAL MUSIC AGENCIES LTD.

A SAILOR'S SONG

1. A man came home from work one night,
   He found his house without a light.
   He went upstairs to go to bed,
   When a saddened thought came to his head.

2. He went into his daughter's room,
   And found her hanging from a beam.
   He took his knife and cut her down,
   And on her breast this note he found.

3. 'My love was for a sailor boy,
   He went to sea, I know not where,
   I always thought his love was true,
   But now I know he does not care.'

4. 'Oh! Lord, I wish my babe was born,
   Then all my troubles would be gone.
   Now dig my grave, both wide and deep,
   And place white lilies at my feet.'

5. He dug her grave both wide and deep,
   And placed white lilies at her feet,
   And on her breast he placed a dove,
   To signify she died for love.

6. Now all you maidens bear in mind,
   A sailor's love is hard to find,
   So if you find one good and true,
   Don't change the old love for the new.

With love
Will
xxx

...d love was for... to sea. I know... thought his love... know he does n... I wish my babe... my troubles would b... and dig my grave... place white lilies both wide... at my fee...
love Ada

The Blind Boy

Andante con espress.
Words by R. Lee. Music by G. W. Moore

VERSE

I am but a poor blind boy, Still my heart is full of joy, Though I never saw the light, Or the flow'rs they call so bright, I can hear the sweet bird sing, And the wild bee on the wing. Bird and bee and summer wind Sing to me be-

CHORUS

-cause I'm blind. They love me, yes, they love me, And to me they are so kind, They love me, yes, they love me, Be-

to verse — cause I am blind. *Fine* — cause I am blind.

Copyright by FRANCIS, DAY & HUNTER LTD., London.

126

THE BLIND BOY

1. I am but a poor blind boy,
   Still my heart is full of joy,
   Though I never saw the light,
   Or the flowers they call so bright,
   I can hear the sweet bird sing,
   And the wild bee on the wing.
   Bird and bee and summer wind
   Sing to me because I'm blind.

   They love me, yes, they love me,
   And to me they are so kind,
   They love me, yes, they love me,
   Because I am blind.

2. With my fingers I can trace
   Every line on mother's face,
   Oft her smile upon me beams,
   I can see it in my dreams;
   Father takes me on his knee,
   Brother's oh so kind to me,
   Sister's arms are round me twined,
   Kisses me because I'm blind.

3. This morning as in bed I lay,
   Mother softly came to pray,
   Said for me such pretty pray'rs,
   And I felt her holy tears
   Falling gently down on me
   And she kissed me, so you see,
   Ev'ryone to me is kind,
   And they love me for I'm blind.

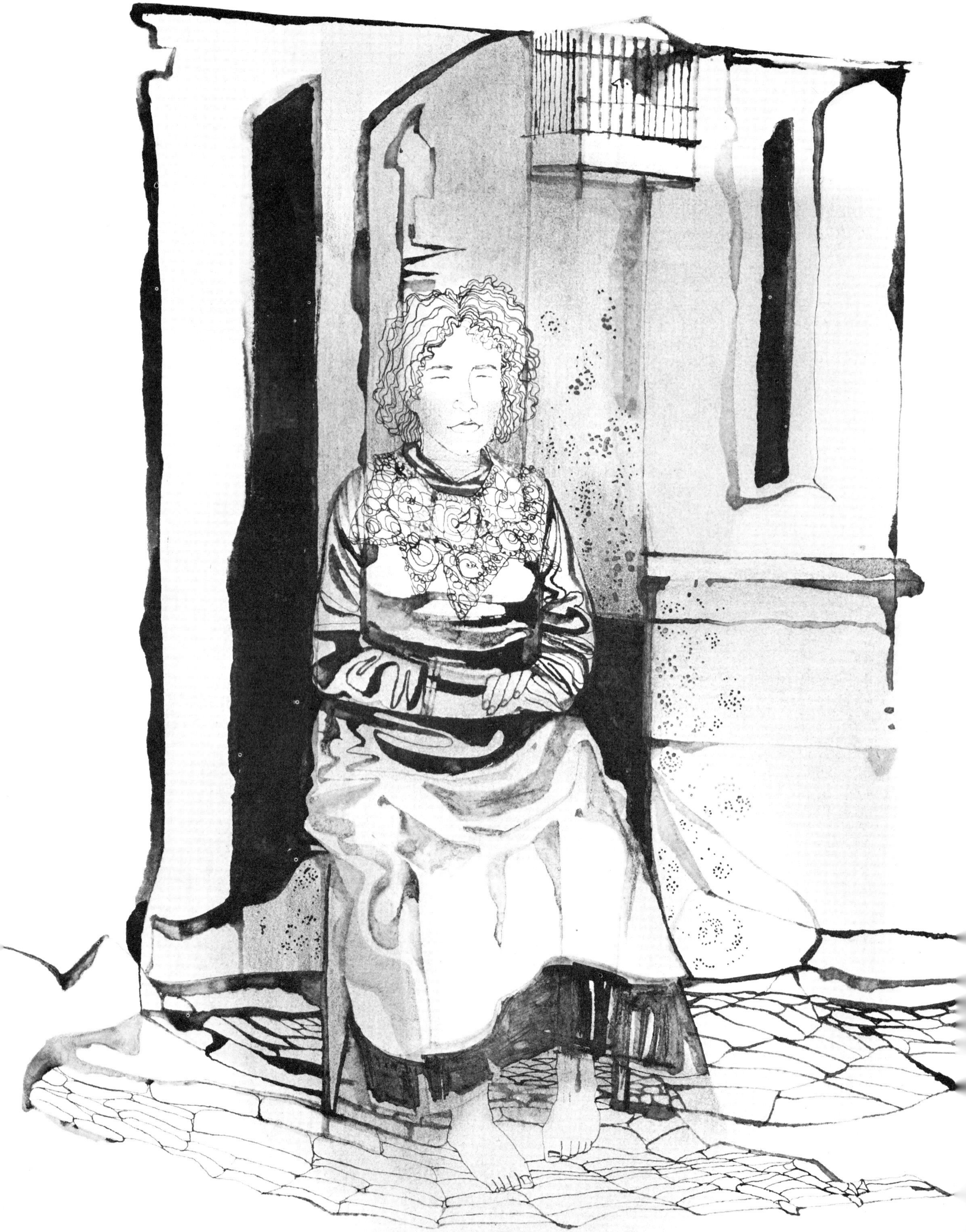

The Blind Irish Girl

Words and music by R. Donnelly

Moderato

The pride of Liss-car-roll is sweet Ka-tie Far-rell, With cheeks as red as ro-ses and teeth as white as pearl; The neigh-bours all pi-ty this col-leen so pret-ty, And, oh! how we all love this blind I-rish girl. The girl

Copyright 1895 by FRANCIS, DAY & HUNTER LTD., London.

THE BLIND IRISH GIRL

1 In my native home, Lisscarroll,
   Lives a colleen who is blind,
   And her name is Katie Farrell,
   To her the neighbours all are kind.
   To see her knit beside her mother
   You ne'er would think her sight was gone—
   And with Barney, her young brother,
   She milks the cows at early dawn.

   The pride of Lisscarroll is sweet Katie Farrell,
   With cheeks as red as roses and teeth as white as pearl;
   The neighbours all pity this colleen so pretty,
   And, oh! how we all love this blind Irish girl.

2 Years ago when she was courting
   Her young sweetheart, Ned Molloy,
   One night they were both out walking,
   With hearts like children full of joy.
   A storm came on and Kate got frightened,
   She seized the arm of sweetheart Ned,
   When both of them were struck by lightning –
   They found her blind, and he was dead.

3 What a sad and awful ending,
   Just when everything seemed bright,
   For her to lose her future husband,
   And she, poor girl, to lose her sight.
   All the neighbours gathered round her,
   One and all to her were kind,
   And the reason – her affliction –
   They pitied her, for she was blind.

Crook 122 NEWINGTON BUTTS, SE

Berkshire Bros 233. ALBERT ROAD SOUTHSEA.

PORTSMOUTH 51. KINGSTON RD J. LONG & SON

Pal of My Cradle Days

Words by Marshall Montgomery. Music by Al Piantadosi

Valse moderato

Pal of my cra - dle days, ___ I've need-ed you al - ways, ___ Since I was a ba - by up - on your knee, You sac - ri - ficed ev - 'ry - thing for me; I stole the gold from your hair, ___ I put the sil - ver threads there, ___ I don't know an - y way, I could ev - er re - pay, Pal of my cra - dle days. days. ___

Copyright 1925 by Leo Feist Inc., New York.
Sub-Publisher: FRANCIS, DAY & HUNTER LTD., London.

PAL OF MY CRADLE DAYS

1 Greatest friend, dearest pal, it was me who caused you
Ev'ry sorrow and heartache you knew.
Your face so fair I have wrinkled with care,
I placed ev'ry line that is there.

> *Pal of my cradle days,*
> *I've needed you always,*
> *Since I was a baby upon your knee,*
> *You sacrificed ev'rything for me;*
> *I stole the gold from your hair,*
> *I put the silver threads there,*
> *I don't know any way,*
> *I could ever repay,*
> *Pal of my cradle days.*

2 What a friend, what a pal, only now I can see
How you dreamed and you planned all for me.
I never knew what a mother goes through
There's nothing that you didn't do.

For I'm Not Coming Home

Collected by Charles Keeping

VERSE
Steadily

As shot and shell were scream-ing, a-cross the bat-tle-field, The boys in blue were fight-ing, their nob-le flag to shield. Then came a cry from their brave Cap-tain, 'Look, lads, our flag is down; Who'll vol-un-teer to save it from dis-grace?' ___ 'I will,' a young boy shout-ed, 'I'll bring it back or die.' Then he fell in-to the thick-est of the fray. ___ He saved the flag but gave his young life, all for his coun-try's sake. And as they brought him back, they heard him say. ___ 'Just

This arrangement © 1975 by BRITISH AND CONTINENTAL MUSIC AGENCIES LTD.

CHORUS

break the news to moth-er, And tell her how I love her, And kiss her dear sweet lips for me, For I'm not com-ing home; Just say there is no oth-er Could take the place of moth-er, And tell her not to wait for me, For I'm not com-ing home.'

FOR I'M NOT COMING HOME

1 As shot and shell were screaming, across the battlefield,
The boys in blue were fighting, their noble flag to shield.
Then came a cry from their brave Captain,
'Look, lads, our flag is down; who'll volunteer to save it from disgrace?'
'I will,' a young boy shouted, 'I'll bring it back or die.'
Then he fell into the thickest of the fray.
He saved the flag but gave his young life, all for his country's sake.
And as they brought him back, they heard him say.

135

*'Just break the news to mother,
And tell her how I love her,
And kiss her dear sweet lips for me,
For I'm not coming home;
Just say there is no other
Could take the place of mother,
And tell her not to wait for me,
For I'm not coming home.'*

2   From afar, a noted General, who witnessed this brave deed,
　　Said 'Who saved the flag? Speak up lads, 'twas nobly brave indeed.'
　　'Here he lies, sir,' said the Captain, 'He's sinking very fast.'
　　And slowly turned away to hide a tear.
　　The General in a moment knelt down beside the boy,
　　Then gave a cry, that touched all hearts that day.
　　'It's my son! My brave young hero, I thought you safe at home.'
　　'Forgive me, father, for I ran away.'

That's What God Made Mothers For

Andante moderato
VERSE

Words and music by Leo Wood

I dreamed I saw my dear old moth-er kiss-ing me good-bye, And though her heart was break-ing and a tear shone in her eye, She whis-pered 'Boy, don't let our part-ing grieve you an-y more, But just re-mem-ber this is what God made all moth-ers for.'

CHORUS

To watch ov-er you when a ba-by, To sing you to sleep with her song,— To try to be near you, to com-fort and cheer you, To teach you the right from the wrong,— To do all she can, just to make you a

Copyright by Meyer Cohen Music Publishing Co., New York.
Sub-Publisher: FRANCIS, DAY & HUNTER LTD., London.

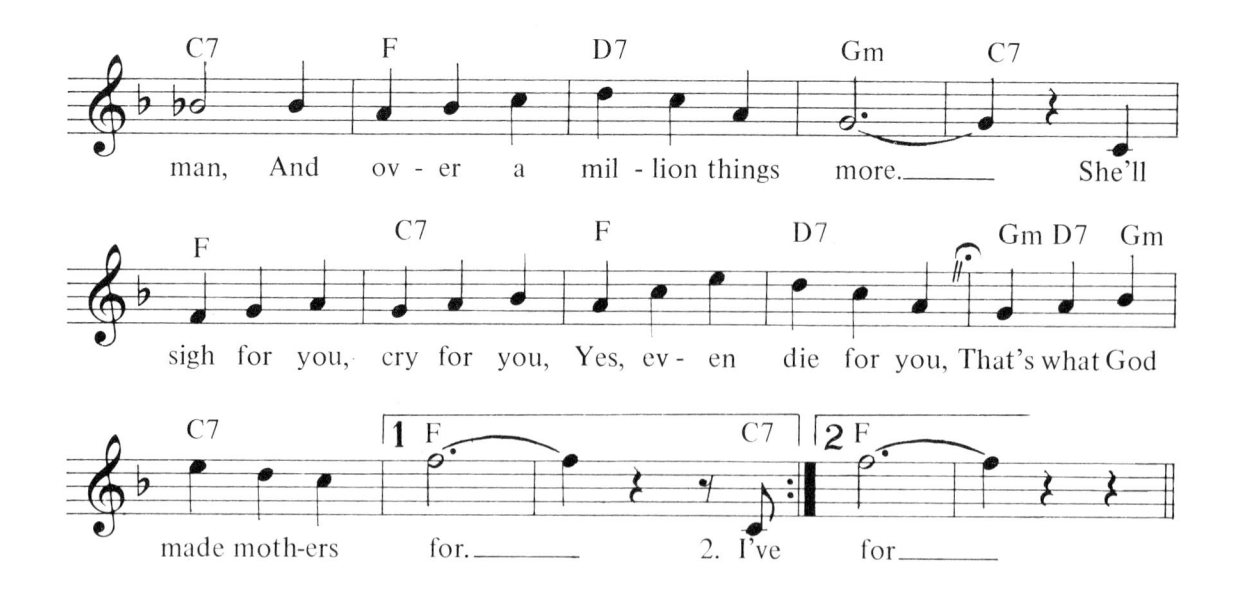

THAT'S WHAT GOD MADE MOTHERS FOR

1. I dreamed I saw my dear old mother kissing me goodbye,
   And though her heart was breaking and a tear shone in her eye,
   She whispered 'Boy, don't let our parting grieve you any more,
   But just remember this is what God made all mothers for.'

   To watch over you when a baby,
   To sing you to sleep with her song,
   To try to be near you, to comfort and cheer you,
   To teach you the right from the wrong,
   To do all she can, just to make you a man,
   And over a million things more.
   She'll sigh for you, cry for you,
   Yes, even die for you,
   That's what God made mothers for.

2. 'I've watched you from the time I rocked you in your cradle, dear;
   I've dreamed for you and planned for you and longed to keep you near;
   But now the time comes, and you're going to some distant shore,
   'Tis only one of the many cares God made all mothers for.'

A. Simmons

238. WESTMINSTER BRIDGE Rd
LONDON. SE.

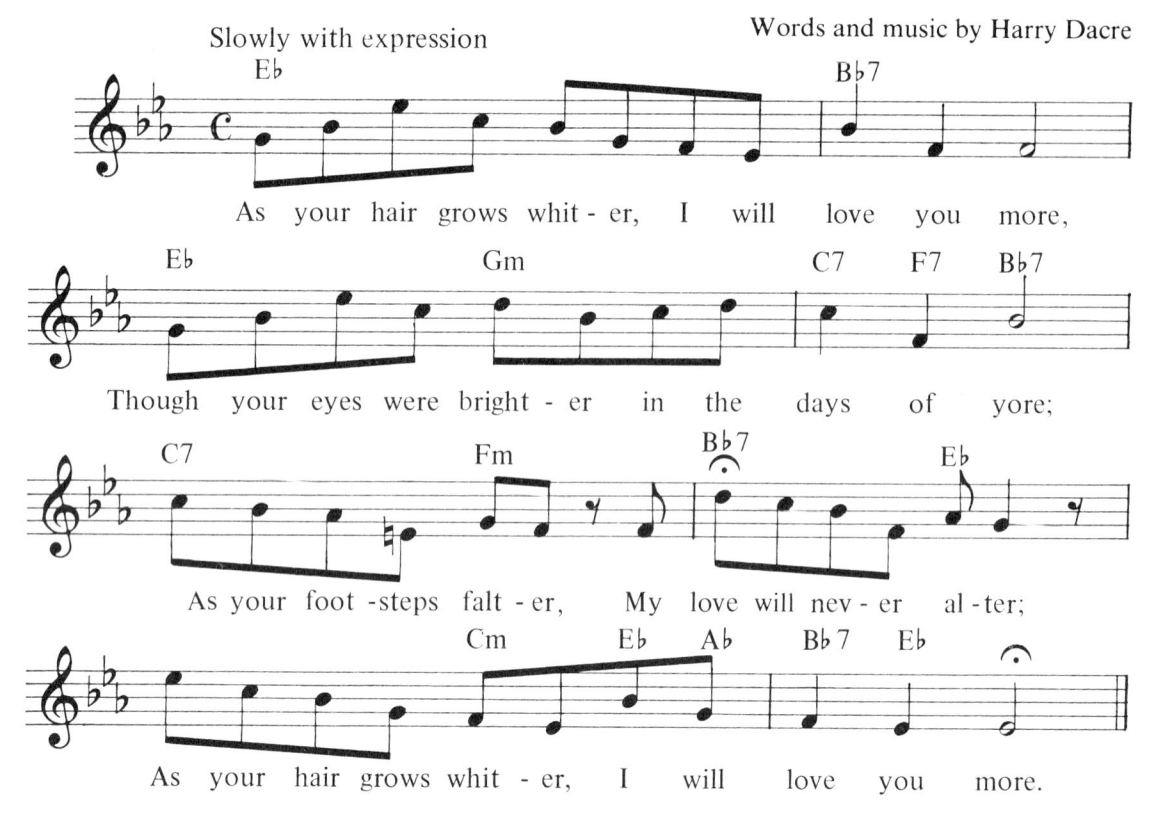

As Your Hair Grows Whiter

Slowly with expression
Words and music by Harry Dacre

As your hair grows whit-er, I will love you more,
Though your eyes were bright-er in the days of yore;
As your foot-steps falt-er, My love will nev-er al-ter;
As your hair grows whit-er, I will love you more.

© Copyright 1897 by Frank Dean & Co.
Copyright assigned 1933 to B. FELDMAN & CO., London, England.

AS YOUR HAIR GROWS WHITER

As your hair grows whiter,
I will love you more,
Though your eyes were brighter in the days of yore;
As your footsteps falter,
My love will never alter;
As your hair grows whiter,
I will love you more.

KNEES-UP SONGS

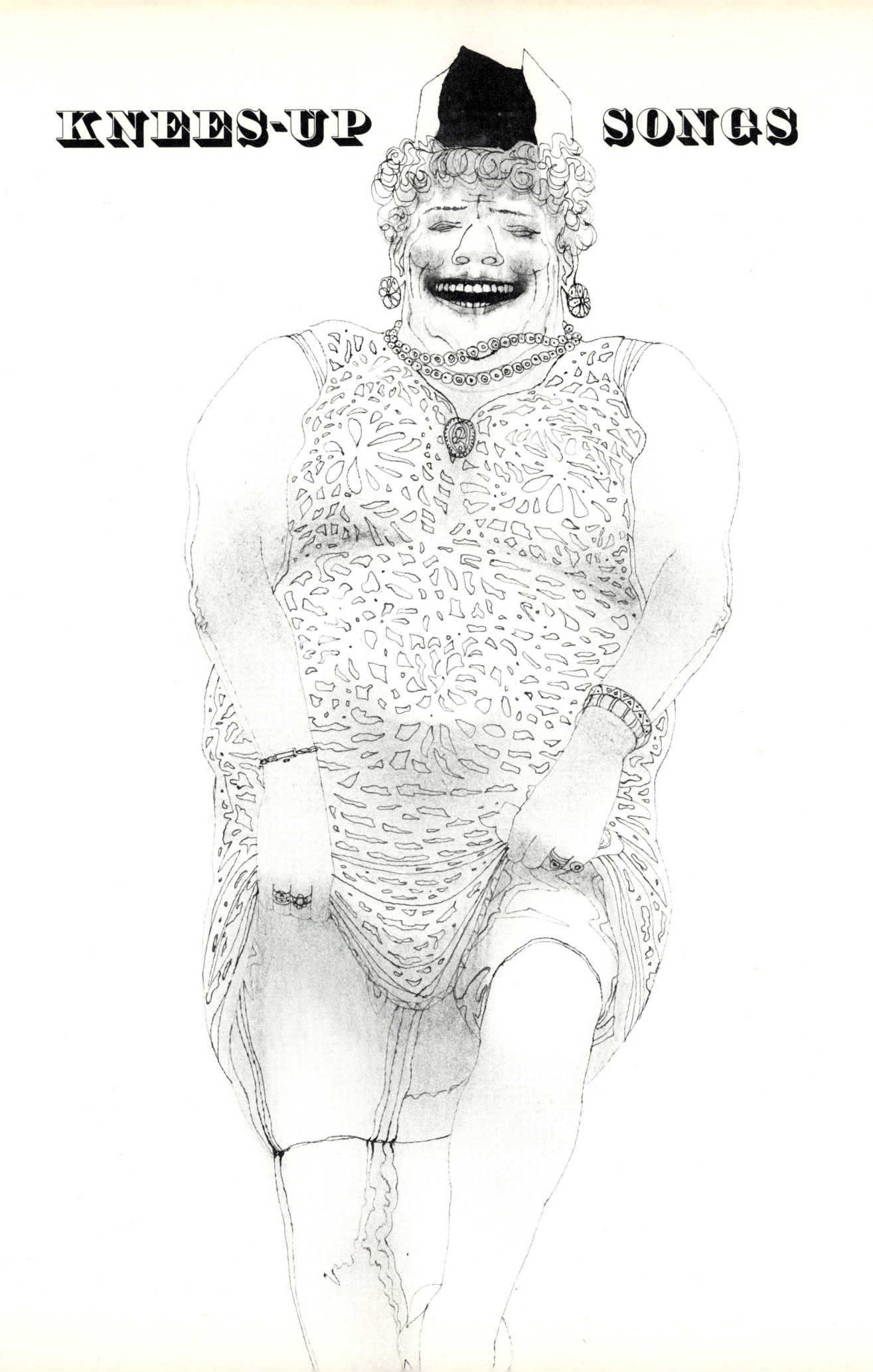

Knees Up Mother Brown!

Bright tempo

Words and music by Harry Weston and Bert Lee

I've just been to a 'ding-dong' down dear old Brixton way, Old Mother Brown the Pearly Queen's a hundred years to-day; Oh! what a cel-e-bra-tion! was proper lah-di-dah! Until they roll'd the carpet up, and shouted 'Nah then, Ma!' (shout)

CHORUS

Knees up Mother Brown! Well! (shout) Knees up Mother Brown! Under the table you must go Ee-i-ee-i-ee-i-oh! If I catch you bending I'll saw your leg right off. So, knees up, knees up!

Copyright 1939 for all Countries by
THE PETER MAURICE MUSIC CO. LTD., London.

Don't get the breeze up Knees up Moth-er Brown. 2. Joe Brown.

KNEES UP MOTHER BROWN!

1 I've just been to a 'ding-dong' down dear old Brixton way,
   Old Mother Brown the Pearly Queen's a hundred years today;
   Oh! what a celebration! was proper lah-di-dah!
   Until they roll'd the carpet up, and shouted 'Nah then, Ma!'

   Knees up Mother Brown! Well! Knees up Mother Brown!
   Under the table you must go
   Ee-i-ee-i-ee-i-oh!
   If I catch you bending
   I'll saw your leg right off.
   So, knees up, knees up!
   Don't get the breeze up
   Knees up Mother Brown.

2 Joe brought his concertina, and Nobby brought the beer,
   And all the little nippers swung upon the chandelier!
   A black-out warden passin' yell'd, 'Ma, pull down that blind,
   Just look at what you're showin'' and we shouted 'Never mind!' Ooh!

   Knees up Mother Brown! Well! Knees up Mother Brown!
   Come a-long dearie let it go!
   Ee-i-ee-i-ee-i-oh!
   It's yer blooming birthday
   Let's wake up all the town!
   So, knees up, knees up!
   Don't get the breeze up
   Knees up Mother Brown.

3 And fat old Uncle 'Enry 'e quite enjoyed the fun,
   The buttons on his Sunday pants kept bustin' one by one!
   But still 'e kept on dancin' – another one went 'pop',
   He said 'I'm goin' ter keep on till me "round-me-'ouses" drop.' Ooh!

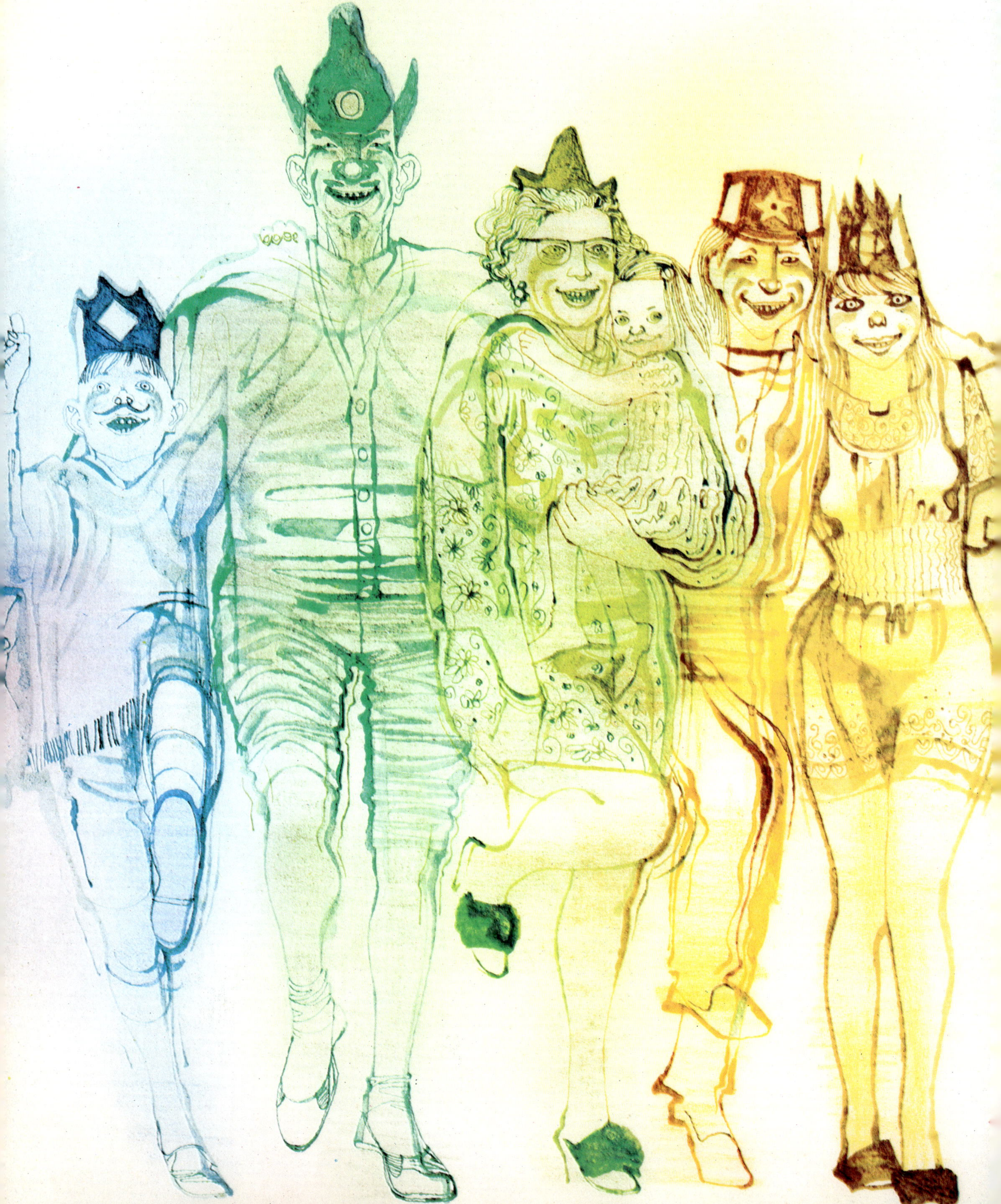

4 Then old Maria Perkins, she danced wiv all 'er might,
Each time she kicked 'er legs up we all shouted with delight,
'Lift up yer skirts Maria – my word, yer doin' fine!
And we can see yer washin' 'anging on the Siegfried Line.' Ooh!

5 We 'ad no 'pig's ear' glasses – but still we didn't mind,
We drank it out of 'vauses' and whatever we could find;
We toasted good ol' Nelson there 'anging by the door
And as we blew the froth at him he shouted with a roar – Ooh!

6 Bill drove up on 'is barrer – just like a proper 'swell'
And Mother Brown said 'Come inside and bring yer moke as well!'
It nibbled Grandad's whiskers, then started kicking out
And as Ma Brown went through the window we began to shout Ooh!

7 And then old Granny Western – she 'ad a good 'blow out',
She 'ad two pints o' winkles wiv some cockles and some stout;
'I might 'ave indigestion,' she murmured wiv a grunt,
'But lummy, up to now, it's all quiet on the 'Western front!' Ooh!

8 A crowd stood round the winder – they 'ad a lovely time,
The kids sat on the railin's, thought it was a pantomime;
Pa went round wiv 'is 'titfer' – collected one and three,
We shouted 'Come on, Mother, show 'em your agilitee.' Ooh!

Any Old Iron?

Words and music by Chas Collins, E.A. Sheppard and Fred Terry

Bright tempo

An-y old iron, an-y old iron, An-y, an-y old, old i-ron? You look neat, talk a-bout a treat, You look dap-per from your nap-per to your feet. Dress'd in style, brand new tile, And your fath-er's old green tie on; But I would-n't give you tup-pence for your old watch chain, Old i-ron, old i-ron! i-ron!

Copyright 1911 by Chas. Sheard & Co.
HERMAN DAREWSKI MUSIC PUBLISHING CO. LTD., London, England.

ANY OLD IRON?

1 Just a week or two ago my poor Old Uncle Bill
  Went and kicked the bucket, and he left me in his will.
  The other day I popp'd around to see poor Auntie Jane,
  She said, 'Your Uncle Bill has left to you a watch and chain.'
  I put it on right across my vest,
  Thought I look'd dandy as it dangled on my chest.
  Just to flash it off I started walking round about,
  A lot of kiddies followed me and all began to shout:

'Any old iron, any old iron,
Any, any old, old iron?
You look neat, talk about a treat,
You look dapper from your napper to your feet.
Dress'd in style, brand new tile,
And your father's old green tie on;
But I wouldn't give you tuppence for your old watch chain,
Old iron, old iron!'

2 I went to the City once and thought I'd have a spree.
   The Mayor of London, he was there, that's who I went to see.
   He dashed up in a canter with a carriage and a pair,
   I shouted, 'Holler boys' and threw my hat up in the air.
   Just then the Mayor he began to smile,
   Saw my face and then he shouted, 'Lummy, what a dial!'
   Started a Lord Mayoring and I thought that I should die
   When pointing to my watch and chain he holler'd to me 'Hi!'

3 Just to have a little bit of fun the other day,
   Made up in my watch and chain, I went and drew my pay.
   Then got out with a lot of other Colonels 'on the loose',
   I got full right up to here in fourp'ny 'stagger juice'.
   One of them said, 'We want a pot of ale.
   Run him to the ragshop and we'll bung him on the scale.'
   I heard the fellow say, 'What's in this bundle that you've got?'
   Then whisper to me kindly: 'Do you want to lose your lot?'

4 Shan't forget when I got married to Selina Brown.
   The way the people laughed at me, it made me feel a clown.
   I began to wonder, when their dials began to crack,
   If by mistake I'd got my Sunday trousers front to back.
   I wore my chain on my darby kell,
   The sun was shining on it and it made me look a swell.
   The organ started playing, and the bells began to ring,
   My chain began to rattle, so the choir began to sing.

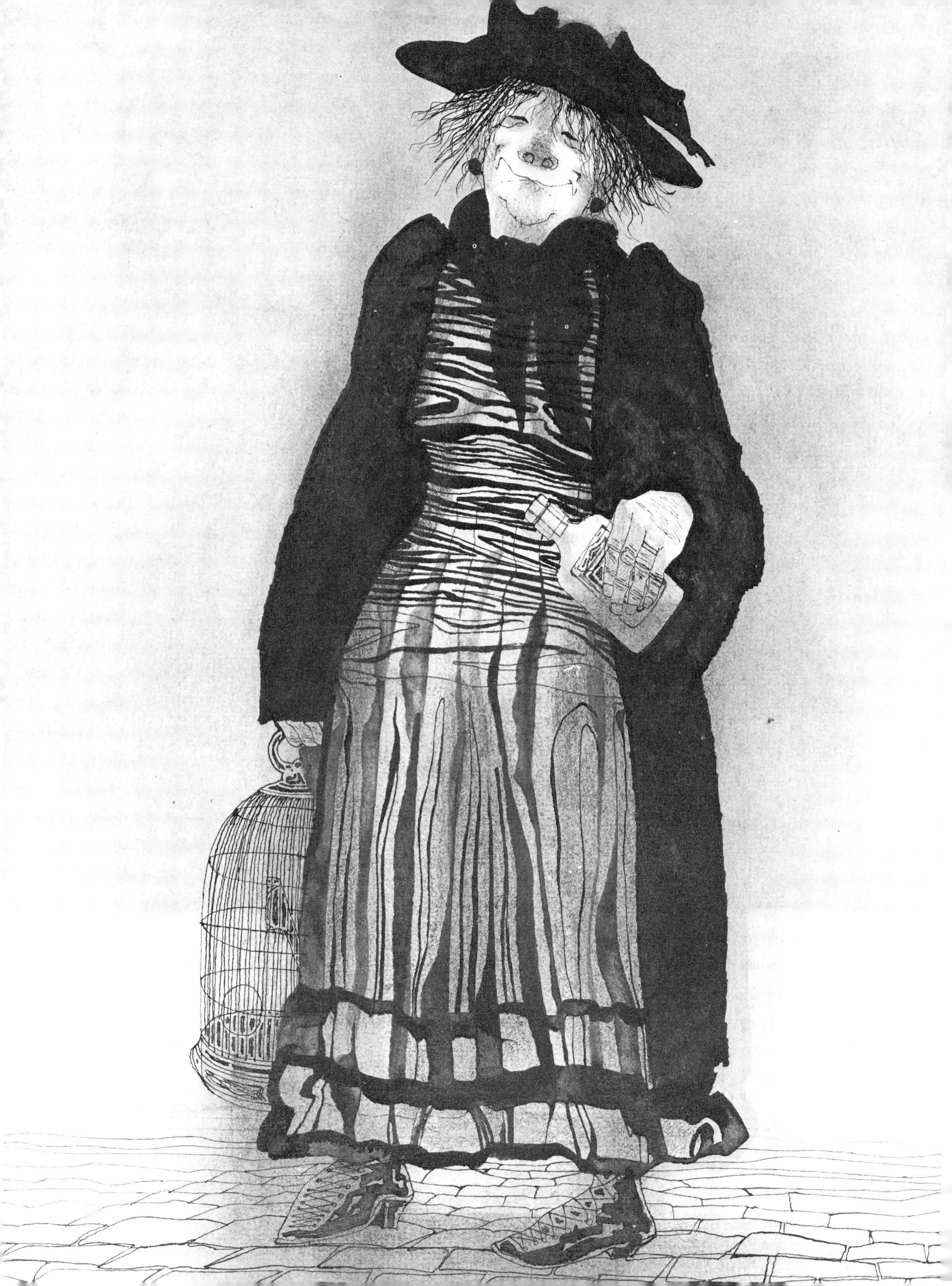

Don't Dilly Dally on the Way

Moderato

Words and music by Charles Collins and Fred W. Leigh

My old man said, 'Fol-low the van, Don't dil-ly dal-ly on the way!' Off went the cart with the home packed in it, I walked be-hind with my old cock lin-net, But I dil-lied and dal-lied, dal-lied and dil-lied, Lost the van and don't know where to roam. I stopped on the way to have the old half-quart-ern, And I can't find my way home.

home.

Copyright by B. FELDMAN & CO., London, England.

DON'T DILLY DALLY ON THE WAY

1 We had to move away
Cos the rent we couldn't pay,
The moving van came round just after dark;
There was me and my old man,
Shoving things inside the van,
Which we'd often done before, let me remark;
We packed all that could be packed
In the van, and that's a fact;
And we got inside all we could get inside,
Then we packed all we could pack
On the tailboard at the back,
Till there wasn't any room for me to ride.

*My old man said, 'Follow the van,
Don't dilly dally on the way!'
Off went the cart with the home packed in it,
I walked behind with my old cock linnet,
But I dillied and dallied, dallied and dillied,
Lost the van and don't know where to roam.
I stopped on the way to have the old
    half-quartern,
And I can't find my way home.*

2 I gave a helping hand
With the marble wash handstand,
And straight we wasn't getting on so bad.
All at once the carman bloke
Had an accident and broke
Well, the nicest bit of china that we had;
You'll understand, of course,
I was cross about the loss
Same as any other human woman would,
But I soon got over that
What with 'two-out' and a chat
Till there wasn't any room for me to ride.

*My old man said, 'Follow the van,
Don't dilly dally on the way!'
Off went the cart with the home packed in it,
I walked behind with my old cock linnet,
But I dillied and dallied, dallied and dillied,
Lost the van and don't know where to roam.
Now who's going to put up the old iron bedstead,
If I can't find my way home?*

3 Oh, I'm in such a mess
I don't know the new address,
Don't even know the blessed neighbourhood,
And I feel as if I might
Have to stay out all the night,
And that ain't a-goin' to do me any good;
I don't make no complaint,
But I'm coming over faint,
What I want now is a good substantial feed,
And I sort o' kind o' feel,
If I don't soon have a meal,
I shall have to rob the linnet of his seed.

*My old man said, 'Follow the van,
Don't dilly dally on the way!'
Off went the cart with the home packed in it,
I walked behind with my old cock linnet,
But I dillied and dallied, dallied and dillied,
Lost the van and don't know where to roam.
You can't trust the 'specials' like the old-time
    'coppers'
When you can't find your way home.*

The Cokey Cokey

Steady tempo

Words and music by Jimmy Kennedy

You put your left arm out, left arm in, Left arm out and shake it all a-bout, You do the Cok-ey Cok-ey, and turn a-round, That's what it's all a-bout.__ You put your right arm out, right arm in, right arm out and shake it all a-bout, You do the Cok-ey Cok-ey, and turn a-round, That's what it's all a-bout.__ You put your bout.__

Copyright 1942 by Kennedy Music Co. Ltd., London.
CAMPBELL, CONNELLY & CO. LTD., London, England for the entire World except U.S.A. & Canada.
Campbell, Connelly Inc., New York, U.S.A. for U.S.A. & Canada.

THE COKEY COKEY

You put your left foot out, left foot in,
Right foot . . . etc.
You put your left hip out, left hip in,
Right hip . . . etc.

151

I've Got a Lovely Bunch of Coconuts

Lively tempo

Words and music by Fred Heatherton

'I've got a lov-e-ly bunch of co-co-nuts,___ There they are a-stand-ing in a row,___ Big ones, small ones, some as big as your head, Give 'em a twist, a flick of the wrist,' That's what the show-man said, 'I've got a lov-e-ly bunch of co-co-nuts;___ Ev-e-ry ball you bowl will make me rich,___ There stands me wife,___ The i-dol of me life, Sing-ing roll or bowl a

Copyright arrangement 1944 & 1948 by the Irwin Dash Music Co. Ltd.
Publication rights for all Countries assigned to BOX & COX (Publications) Ltd., London.

I'VE GOT A LOVELY BUNCH OF COCONUTS

  Down at Barney's Fair–
  One evening I was there,
  When I heard a showman shouting underneath a flare.
  'I've got a lovely bunch of coconuts,
  There they are astanding in a row,
  Big ones, small ones, some as big as your head,
  Give 'em a twist, a flick of the wrist,'
  That's what the showman said,
  'I've got a lovely bunch of coconuts;
  Every ball you bowl will make me rich,
  There stands me wife,
  The idol of me life,
  Singing roll or bowl a ball a penny a pitch,
  Singing roll or bowl a ball a penny a pitch,
  Singing roll or bowl a ball a penny a pitch,
  Roll or bowl a ball,
  Roll or bowl a ball,
  Singing roll or bowl a ball a penny a pitch.'

When There Isn't a Girl About

Brightly

Words and music by Harry Castling and Charles Collins

When there is-n't a girl a-bout you do feel lone-ly, When there is-n't a girl that you can call your on-ly, You're ab-so-lute-ly on the shelf, Don't know what to do with your-self, When there is-n't a girl a-bout. — -bout.

Copyright 1906 by B. FELDMAN & CO., London, England.

WHEN THERE ISN'T A GIRL ABOUT

1 Poor old Robinson Crusoe he had a life of misery,
   There on the island he knew not what to do;
   He'd no girls with loving eyes
   To talk to him and sympathize.
   There on his lonesome things felt awfully blue;
   One night whilst he was shaking up the bed
   He turned to poor old Mister Friday and he said:

'When there isn't a girl about you do feel lonely,
When there isn't a girl that you can call your only,
You're absolutely on the shelf,
Don't know what to do with yourself,
When there isn't a girl about.'

2 Mister Brown was a bachelor and lived in apartments grand,
   On Christmas evening he sat there all alone;
   Just above his head, you know,
   There hung a bunch of mistletoe,
   He stood beneath it and then he gave a groan;
   No sweet maid was near at hand, alas,
   And to himself he whispered, in the looking-glass:

3 Green aboard of a 'P&O' meant to see the world, you know,
   And for a fortnight he quite enjoyed the trip;
   He'd everything that he required
   Ev'rything that he desired,
   Still there was something missing on the ship;
   One day he found what was missing, so
   He murmured to the Captain when he went below:

4 Binks the Bobby was on his beat looking for a snug retreat
   But all the servants were snug beneath the sheets;
   All the clocks were striking four
   And barred was ev'ry airy door,
   Binks seemed deserted, so did all the streets.
   Feeling chilly he crouched against a wall
   And shouted to the man who kept a coffee stall:

I Do Like to Be beside the Seaside

Words and music by John A. Glover-Kind

Con spirito

Oh, I do like to be be-side the sea-side,___ I do like to be be-side the sea.___ I do like to stroll up-on the prom, prom, prom, Where the brass bands play tid-de-ly-om-pom-pom! So just let me be be-side the sea-side,___ I'll be be-side my-self with glee;___ And there's lots of girls be-side, I should like to be be-side, Be-side the sea-side, be-side the sea.___ Oh, I sea.___

Copyright 1909 by B. FELDMAN & CO., London, England.

I DO LIKE TO BE BESIDE THE SEASIDE

1 Everyone delights to spend their summer holiday
   Down beside the side of the silvery sea.
   I'm no exception to the rule, in fact, if I'd my way,
   I'd reside by the side of the silvery sea.
   But when you're just the common or garden Smith or Jones or Brown,
   At bus'ness up in town,
   You've got to settle down.
   You save up all the money you can till summer comes around,
   Then away you go
   To a spot you know,
   Where the cockle shells are found.

Oh, I do like to be beside the seaside,
I do like to be beside the sea.
I do like to stroll upon the prom, prom, prom,
Where the brass bands play tiddely-om-pom-pom!
So just let me be beside the seaside,
I'll be beside myself with glee;
And there's lots of girls beside,
I should like to be beside,
Beside the seaside, beside the sea.

2 Timothy went to Blackpool for the day last Eastertide,
   To see what he could see by the side of the sea;
   Soon as he reached the station there, the first thing he espied
   Was the Wine Lodge door stood open invitingly.
   To quench his thirst, he toddled inside, and called out for a 'wine',
   Which grew to eight or nine,
   Till his nose began to shine.
   Said he, 'What people see in the sea I'm sure I fail to see!'
   So he caught the train
   Back home again
   Then to his wife, said he:

3 William Sykes the burglar, he'd been out to work one night,
   Fill'd his bag with jewels, cash and plate.
   Constable Brown felt quite surprised when William hove in sight,
   Said he: 'The hours you're keeping are far too late.'
   So he grabb'd him by the collar and lodged him safe and sound in jail.
   Next morning looking pale,
   Bill told a tearful tale.
   The judge said, 'For a couple of months I'm sending you away!'
   Said Bill, 'How kind!
   Well if you don't mind
   Where I spend my holiday:

ALTOGETHER SONGS

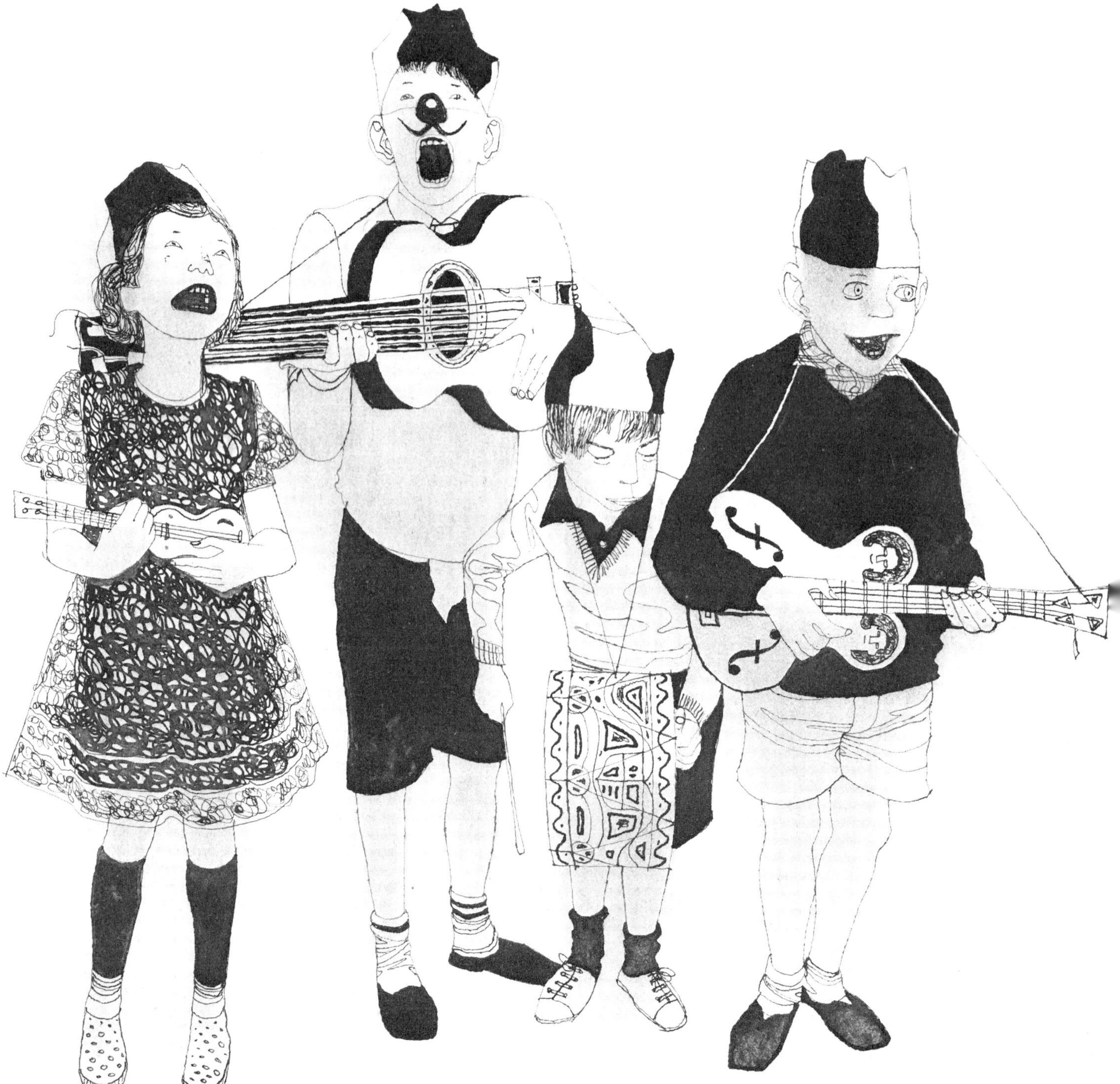

Green Gravel

Collected by Charles Keeping

GREEN GRAVEL

Green gravel, green gravel,
Your grass is so green.
Vicky Keeping, Vicky Keeping,
Your sweatheart is dead.
He sends you a letter,
Concerning bad weather.
Turn your back, you saucy cat,
And say no more to me.

Chase Me Charley

Collected by Charles Keeping

Chase me Char - ley, chase me Char - ley, I lost the leg of my drawers. ___ If you find it, starch and iron it, And give it to one of the boys.

This arrangement © 1975 by BRITISH AND CONTINENTAL MUSIC AGENCIES LTD.

CHASE ME CHARLEY

Chase me Charley, chase me Charley,
I lost the leg of my drawers.
If you find it, starch and iron it,
And give it to one of the boys.

The Naughty Sparrow

Collected by Charles Keeping

This arrangement © 1975 by BRITISH AND CONTINENTAL MUSIC AGENCIES LTD.

THE NAUGHTY SPARROW

1. 'Come in, you naughty bird,
   The rain is falling down.
   What will your mother say,
   If you sit there and drown?
   You are a very naughty bird,
   And never think of me;
   You're certain to be drowned,'
   Said the sparrow on the tree.

2. The little bird was drowned,
   The mother hung her head.
   One morning as I passed,
   I found her lying dead.
   So never say you do not care,
   For don't care it would be,
   You're certain to be drowned,
   Like the sparrow on the tree.

Pack Up Your Troubles in Your Old Kit-bag

Tempo di Marcia

Words by George Asaf. Music by Felix Powell

Pack up your trou-bles in your old kit - bag, And smile, smile, smile. While you've a lu-ci-fer to light your fag, Smile, boys, that's the style. What's the use of wor-ry-ing? It ne-ver was worth-while, so Pack up your trou-bles in your old kit - bag, And smile, smile, smile. smile.

Copyright 1915, in all Countries by FRANCIS, DAY & HUNTER LTD., London.

PACK UP YOUR TROUBLES IN YOUR OLD KIT-BAG

1 Private Perks is a funny little codger
With a smile – a funny smile.
Five feet none, he's an artful little dodger
With a smile – a sunny smile.
Flush or broke, he'll have his little joke,
He can't be suppressed.
All the other fellows have to grin
When he gets this off his chest, Hi!

Pack up your troubles in your old kit-bag,
And smile, smile, smile.
While you've a lucifer to light your fag,
Smile, boys, that's the style.
What's the use of worrying?
It never was worthwhile, so
Pack up your troubles in your old kit-bag,
And smile, smile, smile.

2 Private Perks went amarching into Flanders
With his smile – his funny smile.
He was lov'd by the privates and commanders
For his smile – his sunny smile.
When a throng of Germans came along
With a mighty swing,
Perks yell'd out, 'This little bunch is mine!
Keep your heads down, boys, and sing, Hi!'

3 Private Perks he came back from Bosche shooting
With his smile – his funny smile.
Round his home he then set about recruiting
With his smile – his sunny smile.
He told all his pals, the short, the tall,
What a time he'd had;
And as each enlisted like a man,
Private Perks said, 'Now, my lads, Hi!'

Little Town in My Ould County Down

Words by Richard W. Pascoe. Music by Monte Carlo and Alma M. Sanders

In that dear lit-tle town in the ould Coun-ty Down, It will lin-ger way down in my heart, Tho' it nev-er was grand, it is my fair-y-land, Just a won-der-ful world set a-part. Oh, my Ire-land of dreams, you are with me, it seems, And I care not for fame or re-nown, Like the black sheep of old, I'll come back to the fold, Lit-tle town in the ould Coun-ty

Copyright 1920 by Fred Fisher Inc., 224 West 46th Street, New York.
Sub-Publisher: FRANCIS, DAY & HUNTER LTD., London.

LITTLE TOWN IN MY OULD COUNTY DOWN

1. Sure if I had the wings of a swallow,
   I would travel far over the sea.
   Then a rocky ould road I would follow,
   To a spot that is heaven to me.
   When the sun goes to rest, 'way down in the west,
   Then I'll build such a nest, in the place I love best.

   In that dear little town in the ould County Down,
   It will linger way down in my heart,
   Tho' it never was grand, it is my fairy land,
   Just a wonderful world set apart.
   Oh, my Ireland of dreams, you are with me, it seems,
   And I care not for fame or renown,
   Like the black sheep of old, I'll come back to the fold,
   Little town in the ould County Down!

2. In the evening, when shadows are falling,
   Round the ould door without any key,
   There's a voice in my dreams ever calling,
   There are eyes ever watching for me;
   There is someone I bless with true tenderness,
   And her lips I'll caress, when I bring happiness.

It's a Long, Long Way to Tipperary

Allegro con spirito   Words and music by Jack Judge and Harry Williams

It's a long way to Tip-per-ar-y, It's a long way to go; It's a long way to Tip-per-ar-y, To the sweet-est girl I know! Good-bye Pic-ca-dil-ly, Fare-well Leices-ter Square, It's a long, long way to Tip-per-ar-y But my heart's right there! It's a there!

Copyright 1912 by B. FELDMAN & CO., London, England.

IT'S A LONG, LONG WAY TO TIPPERARY

1 Up to mighty London came an Irishman one day,
As the streets are paved with gold, sure ev'ryone was gay;
Singing songs of Piccadilly, Strand and Leicester Square,
Till Paddy got excited, then he shouted to them there:

   It's a long way to Tipperary,
   It's a long way to go;
   It's a long way to Tipperary,
   To the sweetest girl I know!
   Goodbye Piccadilly,
   Farewell Leicester Square,
   It's a long, long way to Tipperary
   But my heart's right there!

2 Paddy wrote a letter to his Irish Molly O,
Saying, 'Should you not receive it, write and let me know!'
'If I make mistakes in spelling, Molly dear,' said he,
'Remember it's the pen that's bad, don't lay the blame on me.'

3 Molly wrote a neat reply to Irish Paddy O,
Saying, 'Mike Maloney wants to marry me, and so
Leave the Strand and Piccadilly, or you'll be to blame,
For love has fairly drove me silly hoping you're the same.'

Mademoiselle from Armentieres

Words and music by Harry Carlton and J.A. Tunbrid

Copyright 1919 by FRANCIS, DAY & HUNTER LTD., London.

MADEMOISELLE FROM ARMENTIERES

1 What is the latest song the folks are singing around the street,
　Singing around the street,
　Everyone you meet?
　What is the latest melody that's caught the young idea?
　Promise to keep it secret and I'll whisper in your ear:

　　Mademoiselle from Armentieres,
　　Parley vous!
　　Mademoiselle from Armentieres,
　　Same to you!

*Who was the girl that lost her sheep,
Thro' singing this chorus in her sleep?
Mademoiselle from Armentieres.*

2 Sandy McTosh from Glasgow Town he put on his kilts one day,
Down by the briny spray,
Merry and bright and gay,
Out on the Prom he stroll'd along, the wind was rather high,
Who was the girl who turned her head, but only shut one eye?

*Mademoiselle from Armentieres,
Parley vous!
Mademoiselle from Armentieres,
Same to you!
Who was it tied his kilts with string,
To stop 'em doing the Heilan' fling?
Mademoiselle from Armentieres.*

3 Company Sergeant Major Brown was stationed at Aldershot,
All the boys on the spot
Knew that Brown was 'ot;
Even the Colonel had no chance to shine in Cupid's lamp,
Until the day the Tommies spied a stranger in the camp:

*Mademoiselle from Armentieres,
Parley vous!
Mademoiselle from Armentieres,
Same to you!
Giddy old Colonel knows his biz,
And who do you think his batman is?
Mademoiselle from Armentieres.*

4 Up in his aero plane one night went Robinson for a flight,
Everything alright,
Beautiful moonlight night,
Circled around the moon awhile, its wonders to explore,
Looping the loop above the clouds, and what do you think he saw?

*Mademoiselle from Armentieres,
Parley vous!
Mademoiselle from Armentieres,
Same to you!
Who do you think was there in Mars
Adoing the Can-Can to the stars?
Mademoiselle from Armentieres.*

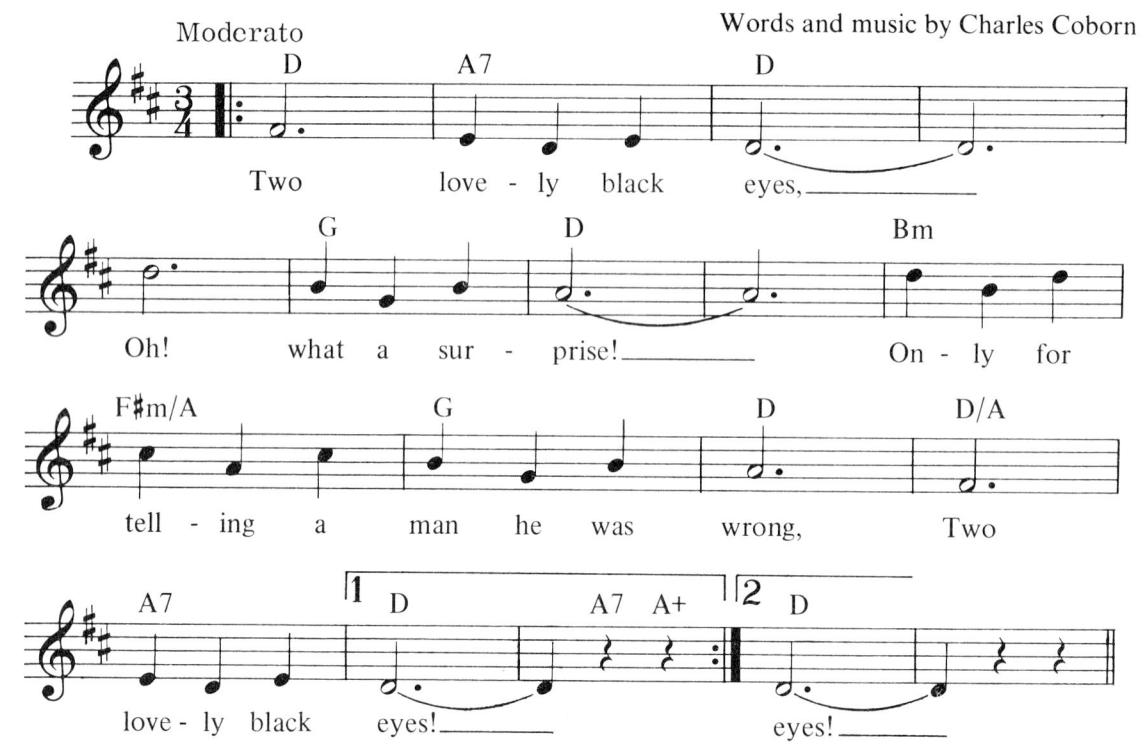

Two Lovely Black Eyes

Moderato
Words and music by Charles Coborn

Two love-ly black eyes, Oh! what a sur-prise! On-ly for tell-ing a man he was wrong, Two love-ly black eyes! eyes!

Copyright by FRANCIS, DAY & HUNTER LTD., London.

TWO LOVELY BLACK EYES

1. Strolling so happy down Bethnal Green,
   This gay youth you might have seen,
   Tompkins and I, with his girl between,
   Oh! what a surprise!
   I praised the Conservatives frank and free,
   Tompkins got angry so speedily,
   All in a moment he handed to me,
   Two lovely black eyes!

   Two lovely black eyes,
   Oh! what a surprise!
   Only for telling a man he was wrong,
   Two lovely black eyes!

2. Next time I argued I thought it best,
   To give the Conservative side a rest,
   The merits of Gladstone I freely press'd,
   When oh! what a surprise!
   The chap I had met was a Tory true,
   Nothing the Liberals right could do,
   This was my share of that argument too,
   Two lovely black eyes!

3. The moral you've caught I can hardly doubt,
   Never on politics rave and shout,
   Leave it to others to fight it out,
   If you would be wise,
   Better, far better, it is to let,
   Liberals and Tories alone, you bet,
   Unless you're willing and anxious to get,
   Two lovely black eyes!

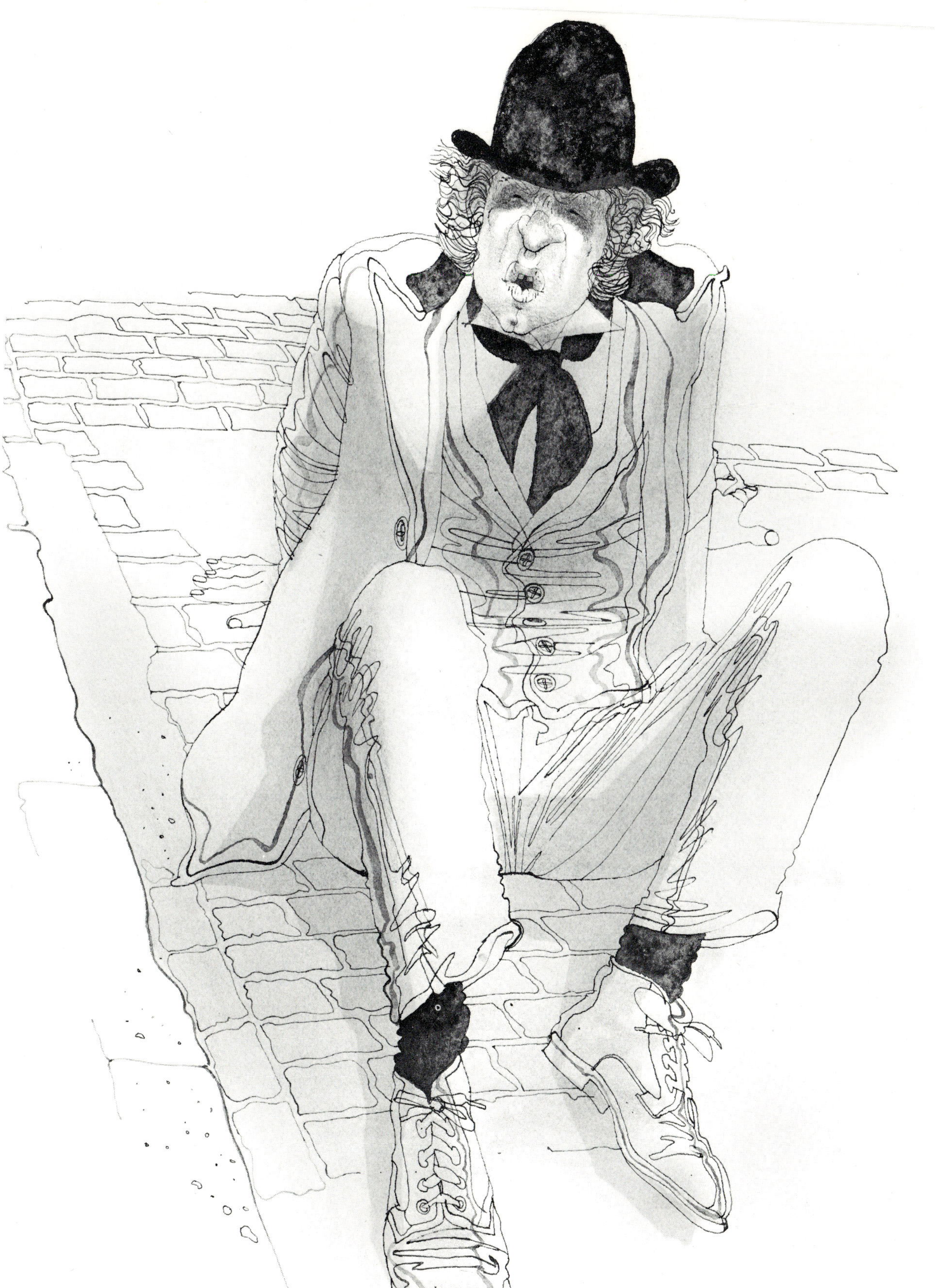

Maybe It's Because I'm a Londoner

Steady tempo

Words and music by Hubert Gregg

May-be it's be-cause I'm a Lon-don-er_____ That I love Lon-don so, May-be it's be-cause I'm a Lon-don-er_____ That I think of her_____ where-ev-er I go._____ I get a fun-ny feel-ing in-side of me_____ Just walk-ing up and down,_____ May-be it's be-cause I'm a Lon-don-er That I love Lon-don Town. Town

Copyright 1947 by FRANCIS, DAY & HUNTER LTD., London.

MAYBE IT'S BECAUSE I'M A LONDONER

Maybe it's because I'm a Londoner
That I love London so,
Maybe it's because I'm a Londoner
That I think of her wherever I go.
I get a funny feeling inside of me
Just walking up and down,
Maybe it's because I'm a Londoner
That I love London Town.

Glorious Beer

Moderato

Words by Steve Leggett. Music by Will Godwin

Beer, beer, glo-ri-ous beer! Fill your-selves right up to here! Drink a good deal of it, make a good meal of it, Stick to your old-fash-ioned beer! Don't be a-fraid of it, drink till you're made of it, Now all to-geth-er, a cheer! Up with the sale of it, down with a pail of it, Glo-ri-ous, glo-ri-ous beer! beer!

Copyright by FRANCIS, DAY & HUNTER LTD., London.

GLORIOUS BEER

1. Now I won't sing of sherbet and water,
   For sherbet and beer will not rhyme;
   The working mán can't afford champagne,
   It's a bit more than two 'D' a time,
   So I'll sing you a song of a gargle,
   A gargle that I love so dear,
   I allude to that grand institution,
   That beautiful tonic called beer, beer, beer.

   Beer, beer, glorious beer!
   Fill yourselves right up to here!
   Drink a good deal of it, make a good meal of it,
   Stick to your old-fashioned beer!
   Don't be afraid of it, drink till you're made of it,
   Now all together, a cheer!
   Up with the sale of it, down with a pail of it,
   Glorious, glorious beer!

2. It's the daddy of all lubricators,
   The best thing there is for the neck;
   Can be used as a gargle or lotion
   By persons of every sect;
   Now we know who the goddess of wine was,
   But was there a goddess of beer?
   If so, let us drink to her health, boys,
   And wish that we'd just got her here, here, here!

3. So up, up with brandies and sodas,
   But down, down and down with the beer;
   It's good for you when you are hungry,
   You can eat it without any fear;
   So mop up the beer while you're able,
   Of four-half let's all have our fill,
   And I know you'll all join me in wishing
   Good luck to my dear uncle Bill, Bill, Bill!

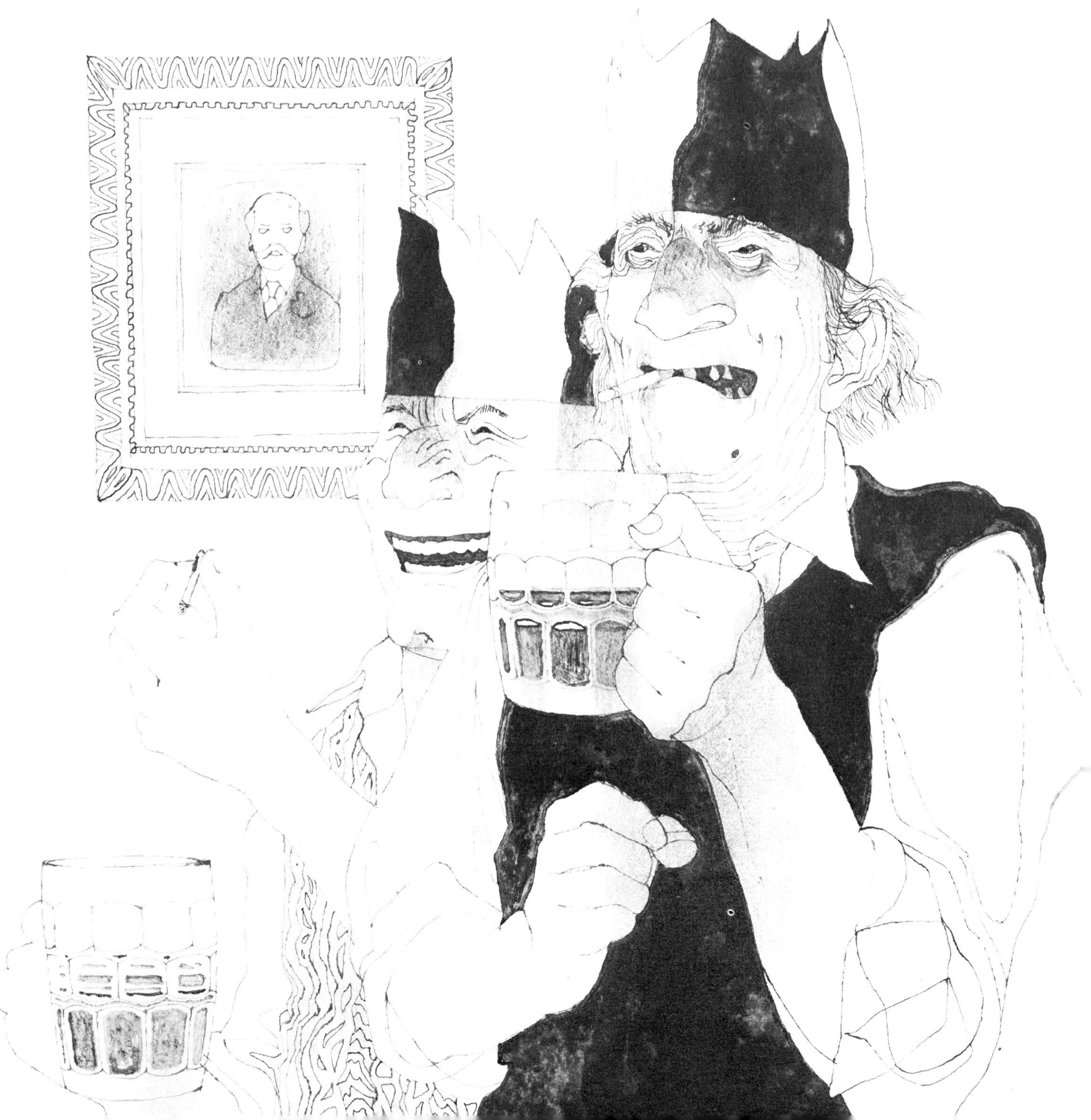

Come Inside, Yer Silly Bugger

Collected by Charles Keeping

Come inside, yer silly bugger, come inside,
I thought you 'ad a bit more sense.
Working for yer living? Take my tip:
Act a bit stupid, and become a lunatic.
You get your meals quite regular,
And three new suits beside;
Thirty bob a week, no wife and kids to keep,
Come inside, yer silly bugger, come inside.

This arrangement © 1975 by BRITISH AND CONTINENTAL MUSIC AGENCIES LTD.

COME INSIDE, YER SILLY BUGGER

Come inside, yer silly bugger, come inside,
I thought you 'ad a bit more sense.
Working for yer living? Take my tip:
Act a bit stupid, and become a lunatic.
You get your meals quite regular,
And three new suits beside;
Thirty bob a week, no wife and kids to keep,
Come inside, yer silly bugger, come inside.

We All Came in the World with Nothing

Moderato
Collected by Charles Keeping

We all came in the world with nothing, No clothes to wear, Bear in mind, you will find All your troubles you will leave behind. You finished up just the same as you began, Without the slightest doubt, Well, we all came in the world with nothing And we can't take anything out.

Copyright by B. FELDMAN & CO., London, England.

WE ALL CAME IN THE WORLD WITH NOTHING

1. We all came in the world with nothing,
   No clothes to wear,
   Bear in mind, you will find
   All your troubles you will leave behind.

2. You finished up just the same as you began,
   Without the slightest doubt.
   Well, we all came in the world with nothing
   And we can't take anything out.

PARTING SONGS

We All Go the Same Way Home

Tempo di Marcia
Words and music by C.W. Murphy and Harry Castling

We all go the same way home,
All the whole col-lec-tion in the same di-rec-tion,
All go the same way home, So there's no need to part at all.
We all go the same way home, Let's be gay and heart-y, don't break up the part-y,
We'll cling to-geth-er like the i-vy, On the old gar-den wall. We wall.

Copyright by FRANCIS, DAY & HUNTER LTD., London.

WE ALL GO THE SAME WAY HOME

1 The wedding day was over, and the party breaking up,
All the guests were making for the door,
And as they danced along the hall like children on the sands,
The bride and bridegroom stood there holding hands.
The company wished the couple health and wealth, too,
And were dispersing in twos and threes,
When Johnson through the din and noise
Cried to all the girls and boys,
'Come, come, get together please!'

We all go the same way home,
All the whole collection in the same direction,
All go the same way home,
So there's no need to part at all.
We all go the same way home,
Let's be gay and hearty, don't break up the party,
We'll cling together like the ivy,
On the old garden wall.

2 A rajah gay was trav'lling back to India once again,
With his four and twenty little wives,
In one compartment of the train with all of them he got,
To keep his jealous eye upon the lot.
A porter shouted 'Hi! you're overcrowding,
There's room for ten here, not twenty-four.'
The rajah answered, 'We're all right,
Though we're packed in rather tight,
Don't you worry any more!'

3 When Noah looked from the ark one day and found the rain had stopped,
And the streets were beautiful and dry,
Said he, 'I haven't had a stroll for forty days or more,'
Then out he went and never shut the door.
The animals came tramping down the gangway,
The alligator, the kangeroo,
A blue-faced monkey led the throng,
Screaming as they marched along
'Hi! Hi! this way for the Zoo!'

4   Just by the House of Commons stood a band of Suffragettes,
    And the lot were screaming for 'The Vote',
    When all at once there came a crowd of gentlemen in blue,
    And very quickly captured all the crew.
    The prison van was ordered from the station,
    And soon the ladies were far from gay.
    The driver cracked his whip and cried,
    When the lot were packed inside,
    'Last bus girls for Holloway!'

Fall In and Follow Me

1   Mister Gibson, once a Military man,
    Uses Military language when he can;
    Once he left his quiet suburban nest,
    With six pals he went up west.
    Said the others, 'Now, what shall we do?
    As we want some fun, we'll leave it all to you.'
    Then Gibson swelled with Military pride,
    Twirling his moustache he cried:

2   Off they went to see a ballet gay that night,
    And the lovely dancing girls gave them delight;
    Then behind the scenes they thought they'd go,
    Said, 'Those girls we'd like to know.'
    Gibson quickly led the way, you're sure,
    Through a passage dark until they reached a door
    And then he stopped and whispered low, 'I guess
    This is where the fairies dress.'

3   Something after twelve they started home again,
    Had to walk, they'd lost the last suburban train;
    By the old canal they tramped along,
    Singing out the latest song.
    Then they saw their wives, oh! what a scream!
    Walking up towards them by the flowing stream;
    Then Gibson slipped and fell into the tide,
    Splashed about and loudly cried:

FALL IN AND FOLLOW ME

Tempo di Marcia
CHORUS

Words by A.J. Mills. Music by Bennett Scott

Fall in and follow me! Fall in and follow me! Come along and never mind the weather, All together, stand on me, boys, I know the way to go, I'll take you for a spree, You do as I do and you'll do right, Fall in and follow me! me!

Copyright 1910, in England and America by THE STAR MUSIC PUBLISHING CO. LTD. All Rights Reserved.

Memories

Moderato Words by Gustave Kahn. Music by Robert van Alstyne

Mem - o - ries, mem - o - ries, Dreams of love so true. O'er the Sea of Mem - o - ry I'm drift - ing back to you. Child - hood days, wild - wood days, A - mong the birds and bees You left me a - lone, But still you're my own In my beau - ti - ful mem - o - ries. ries.

Copyright 1915 by Jerome H. Remick & Co., New York.
Sub-Publisher: FRANCIS, DAY & HUNTER LTD., London.

MEMORIES

1 Round me at twilight come stealing
   Shadows of days that are gone,
   Dreams of the old days revealing
   Mem'ries of love's golden dawn.

   Memories, memories,
   Dreams of love so true.
   O'er the Sea of Memory
   I'm drifting back to you.
   Childhood days, wildwood days,
   Among the birds and bees
   You left me alone,
   But still you're my own
   In my beautiful memories.

2 Sunlight may teach me forgetting,
   Noonlight bring thoughts that are new,
   Twilight brings sighs and regretting,
   Moonlight means sweet dreams of you.

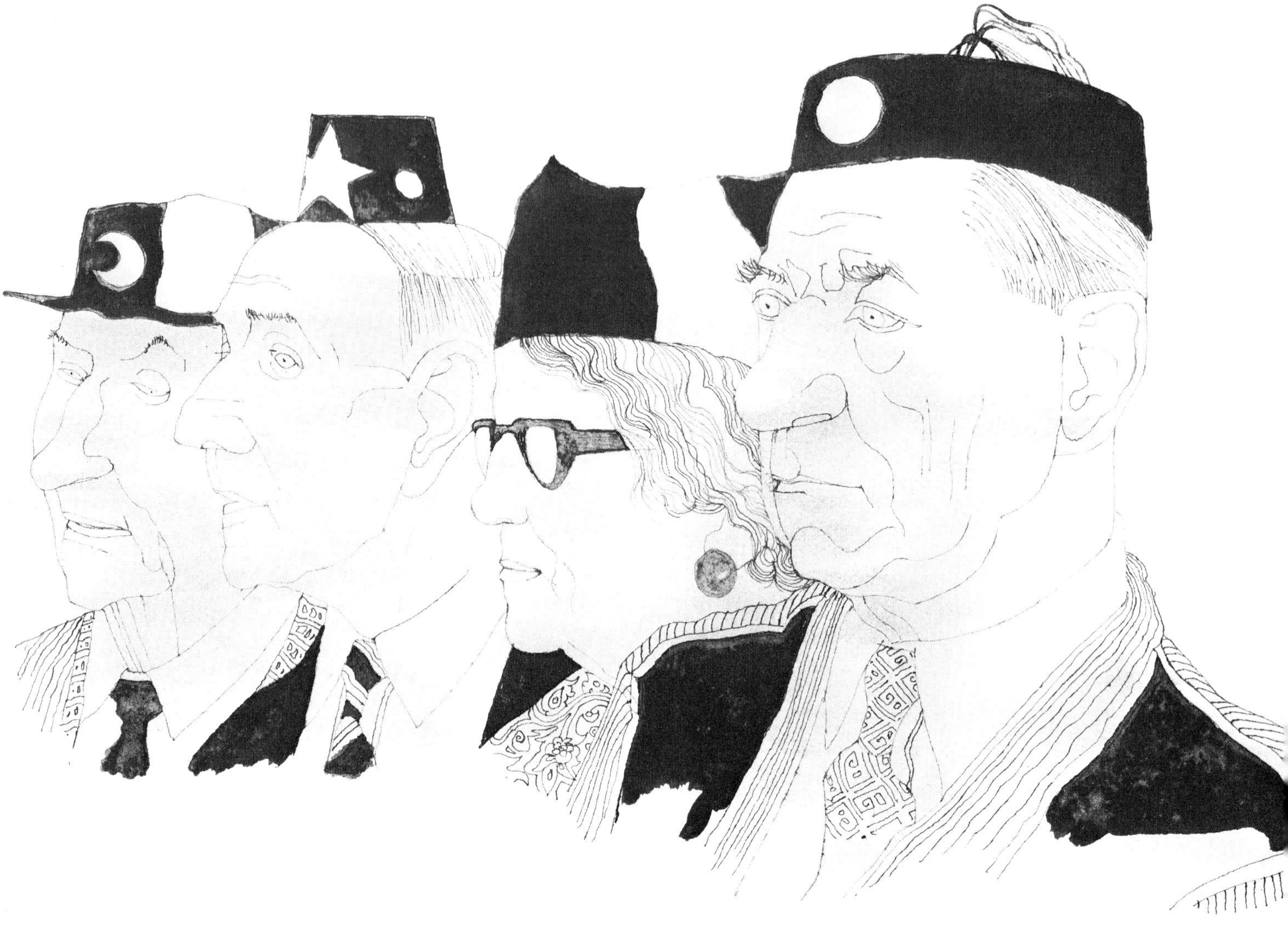

Index of Titles

'Alf a Pint of Ale	22
The Amateur Whitewasher	78
Any Old Iron?	146
As Your Hair Grows Whiter	140
The Blind Boy	126
The Blind Irish Girl	129
Boiled Beef and Carrots	72
Chase Me Charley	162
The Cokey Cokey	151
Come Inside, Yer Silly Bugger	179
A Comical Cock	74
The Coster's Linnet	112
The D.C.M.	43
Don't Dilly Dally on the Way	149
Down the Road	24
Fall In and Follow Me	184
Feeding the Ducks on the Pond	82
For I'm Not Coming Home	134
Glorious Beer	176
The Golden Dustman	18
Granny	100
Green Gravel	161
The Hobnailed Boots that Farver Wore	11
I Do Like to Be beside the Seaside	156
If It Wasn't For the 'Ouses In Between	47
If Those Lips Could Only Speak	91
I'm a Navvy	81
I'm Henery the Eighth, I Am!	67
In the Shade of the Old Apple Tree	50
I Speak the Truth	118
It's a Great Big Shame	32
It's a Long, Long Way to Tipperary	168
I've Got a Lovely Bunch of Coconuts	152
Jeerusalem's Dead!	107
Knees Up Mother Brown!	142
Little Town in My Ould County Down	166
Liza, It's a Beautiful Starry Night	87
Liza Johnston	90
Liza, You Are a Lady	86
Mademoiselle from Armentieres	170
Maybe It's Because I'm a Londoner	174
Memories	186
The Moon Shines Tonight on Charlie Chaplin	76
My London Country Lane	28
My Old Dutch	116
The Naughty Sparrow	163
On Monday I Never Go to Work	64
Pack Up Your Troubles in Your Old Kit-Bag	164
Pal of My Cradle Days	132
A Sailor's Song	124
Silver Bells	110
Sing Me to Sleep	70
The Song of the Thrush	122
Sons of the Sea	98
The Sunshine of Your Smile	96
That's What God Made Mothers For	137
That's Where My Love Lies Dreaming	93
They're All Very Fine and Large	61
They're Moving Father's Grave to Build a Sewer	52
Two Lovely Black Eyes	172
We All Came in the World with Nothing	180
We All Go the Same Way Home	182
What a Mouth!	14
When I Went for a Soldier	84
When the Old Dun Cow Caught Fire	37
When There Isn't a Girl About	154
When the Summer Comes Again	102
Where Did You Get That Hat?	58
Whilst the Dance Goes On	105
Wot Cher!	54
Wot's the Good of Hanyfink! Why! Nuffink!	34

Index of First Lines

A man came home from work one night	124
Amidst a scene of great splendour	106
As shot and shell were screaming, across the battlefield	135
As your hair grows whiter	140
Chase me Charley, chase me Charley	162
Come inside, yer silly bugger, come inside	179
Come in, you naughty bird	163
Dear face that holds so sweet a smile for me	97
Down at Barney's Fair	153
Everyone delights to spend their summer holiday	157
Feeding the ducks on the pond (Quack! Quack!)	83
For the moon shines tonight on Charlie Chaplin	77
Green gravel, green gravel	161
Have you heard the talk of foreign pow'rs	98
He stood in a beautiful mansion	92
I am but a poor blind boy	127
I 'ate those blokes wot talk about	23
I dreamed I saw my dear old mother kissing me goodbye	138
If you saw my little backyard, 'Wot a pretty spot' you'd cry	47
I know an old-fashioned lady	101
I'm a navvy, I'm a navvy, working on the line	81
I'm a very handy man	79
I'm full of joy, I'm full of joy	120
In my native home, Lisscarroll	129
In the hush of eventide	110
I've 'ad four 'arf-pints at the 'Magpie-an'-Stump'	109
I've got a pal	117
I've just been to a 'ding-dong' down dear old Brixton way	143
I've lost my pal, 'e's the best in all the tahn	33
Jimmy Binks would be a handsome feller	15
Just a week or two ago my poor old Uncle Bill	146
Last week down our alley come a toff	54
Liza, it's a beautiful starry night	87
Liza, you are a lady	86
Liza, you are my donna	90
Maybe it's because I'm a Londoner	175
Me and old Bill Smiff's bin dust-'oys	18
Mister Gibson, once a Military man	184
Now how I came to get this hat, 'tis very strange and funny	59
Now I have to live in London, bricks and mortar ev'rywhere	28
Now I won't sing of sherbert and water	177
Oh an Englishman, a Frenchman and a Hebrew	51
Oh, they're moving father's grave to build a sewer	53
Oh! won't we have some money, Nell	103
One Sunday afternoon	75
On Monday I never go to work	65
Pal of my cradle days	133
Poor Farver's feet took up half the street	11
Poor old Robinson Crusoe he had a life of misery	154
Private Perks is a funny little codger	165
Round me at twilight come stealing	187
Since first I copp'd a tidy lump o' swag	26
Sing me to sleep I heard a man bawl	71
Some pals and I in a public house	37
Strolling so happy down Bethnal Green	172
Sure if I had the wings of a swallow	167
That's where my love lies dreaming	93
The wedding day was over, and the party breaking up	183
This world's a disappointment, yuss!	35
To be too modest nowadays	61
Up to mighty London came an Irishman one day	169
We all came in the world with nothing	180
We had to move away	150
What is the latest song the folks are singing around the street	170
When I was a nipper only six months old	73
When I went for a soldier	84
Years ago out in the wilds of Australia	123
You don't know who you're looking at; now have a look at me!	67
You never know what you can do till you're put to the test	43
You put your left arm out, left arm in	151
You've all heard of Liza's wedding	114